Wise Guide Enrichment Activity Worksheets: Lists N-Z

Student Worksheets & Teacher Answer Keys
for Wanda Sanseri's
Spell to Write and Read

Elizabeth FitzGerald, M.S.

LITHBTH Educational Services
Hayward, CA

Wise Guide Enrichment Activity Worksheets: Lists N-Z

LITHBTH Educational Services
California

Third Printing

Cover Art by David FitzGerald

Illustrated by Shannon and Elizabeth FitzGerald

www.swrtraining.com

ISBN 978-0-9744920-3-2

PRINTED IN THE UNITED STATES OF AMERICA

Dedicated to Liza

As a high school student,
you wrestled with learning English,
your second language,
in a way you'd never learned it before.

You worked hard.
You trusted me.
You thrived.

And then the day came that I gave you
the longest word in the language.
You paused and looked at me like I was crazy,
but you also thought about it.
As a confident smile spread across your face,
you said, "I've got this.
It's nothing but phonograms
and little syllables, right?
Let's do this!"

And so you did.

Wise Guide Enrichment Activity Worksheets

Table of Contents

Lists N-1 to N-8 (con't)

Lists O-1 to O-6

Key to Language Arts Category Codes

The activities in *The Wise Guide* fall into different categories for language learning and other curricular subjects. Many activities qualify for more than one category.

A	Art
B	Bible
D	Diagramming
G	Grammar
Geo	Geography
L	Listening
Ph	Phonograms
P	Punctuation
V	Vocabulary
W	Writing
WB	Word-building

Foreword

Liz FitzGerald has created this helpful supplement for *The Wise Guide for Spelling* with my blessing. Going back to the days when my *Teaching Reading at Home and School* was crafted as a supplement to *Writing Road to Reading*, she became my second Endorsed Teacher Trainer. Her feedback and editing were invaluable as I transformed that work into the stand-alone program that *Spell to Write and Read* is today. Her professional training as a Speech and Language Therapist helped me understand and articulate more clearly concepts like "think-to-spell" and coarticulation. She has had a long, dedicated track record of working with the program. In addition to teaching many SWR seminars over the years, she developed the award-winning *Cursive First* program. For many years, she has been the faithful owner and moderator of the SWR Yahoo Support Group that today has over thirty-five hundred members. She has created a dynamic web site that helps explain the program and provide practical help. Her consistent dedication has helped her sense the pulse of SWR users and given her a heart to address the needs she sees.

Liz has worked to harmonize her vision for this project directly with me. She sought my permission to do the worksheets. She has provided working rough draft copies for my review and honored my suggestions. I am strongly pleased with the results. This is a powerful addition to the program. I believe this valuable resource will meet a great need for the busy educator who wants to take the fullest advantage of the various spelling enrichments in *The Wise Guide*.

Happy Teaching,

Wanda Sanseri
author of *Spell to Write and Read*

Foreword

Preface

After grad school for Speech and Language Pathology, my first full-time position was as a Special Day Class Teacher for severe speech and language delayed children. With the goal of learning how to teach probably the most important subject taught in the classroom, I immediately enrolled in a graduate level training class called "How to Teach Reading." In that class I learned reading theory, group management, and that once a student could learn to decode the written text, teaching reading was really all about teaching language. As a language therapist, I found myself in familiar territory. However, I didn't learn how to unlock the mysteries of the English written code for young students until I took Wanda Sanseri's Basic Seminar for the method that would become known as Spell to Write and Read.

At the time I started teaching with Wanda's materials, we were using *The Writing Road to Reading,* and the only reinforcement activity I could assign my students was to write their spelling words in sentences; an important task, but by no means a thorough language experience. When Wanda published *The Wise Guide for Spelling* in 2000, it was filled with ideas and activities that used the spelling words as a springboard for all sorts of language learning. As we worked through the Wise Lists, my students' vocabularies and their understanding of base words and derivatives also advanced. This led to better reading comprehension as they were able to understand what they were reading and how to decode unfamiliar words. They recognized long "complicated" words as nothing but phonograms and simple syllables, all following our reliable rules.

While working with teachers in my seminars and interacting with our program users on our Yahoo Support Group, I started noticing a pattern. These teachers loved the program and the beauty of the multi-sensory approach. They worked to perfect their spelling dictation and to navigate the weekly lessons. However, they tended to overlook or skip the reinforcement activities. Their focus was merely on teaching new spelling words because they didn't have the time nor did they see the value of setting up and working through the enrichment lessons. When teachers would question why their students were not advancing as they hoped, I discovered a common denominator; they were not taking full advantage of the language lessons in *The Wise Guide*. Their students were rarely being given the opportunity to experience their spelling words in the context of the language they were expected to use for everyday reading and writing activities.

In 2012 I returned to the classroom to start teaching SWR one or two days a week. Naturally, I wanted to take full advantage of the rich bounty that *The Wise Guide* held. Since I was not working with the students every day, I developed worksheets for *The Wise Guide* activities so my students could practice their spelling words in a variety of meaningful ways, all while continuing to reinforce the multi-sensory approach. The worksheets had to be easy to understand for both the student and the parent. They incorporated grammar instruction, something teachers often feel inadequate to teach. Eventually, the material included all of the Wise Lists from A-Z. When I had my seminar students try them out, they wanted their own copies so they, too, could strengthen their language arts instruction.

My sincere gratitude goes to my Foundational Language Arts students and parents at HEART Academy, and to the Cunningham, DiNatale, Boyum, and Orelup families. Without your faithful field-testing, I would only have ideas swirling around in my head and no finished materials with which to bless other

SWR students and teachers. I am indebted to Wanda Sanseri for teaching me how to teach reading and spelling. She entrusted me with her program as one of her Endorsed Trainers, and she continues to invest in my life as an educator and as a daughter of the King.

May you yield rich rewards for your investment in our next generation,

Liz

Elizabeth FitzGerald, M.S.
Endorsed SWR Trainer, Northern CA

How to Use These Worksheets

I. WORKSHEET DESIGN & PURPOSE

1. **Worksheet activities match the instructions found in *The Wise Guide* ©2015**. Previous versions of *The Wise Guide* can easily be used! Just be aware there may be new activities listed in this book or changes in activity examples that aren't in an older book.

2. **If an assignment lends itself to a worksheet, it's included.**
   a. Worksheets are meant to supplement the activities in The Wise Guide, NOT to replace it. You need both!
   b. Sentence Writing Activities are included only when they are specifically reinforcing a concept just taught or where a new concept is introduced. Most sentence writing assignments can easily take place on regular paper, so a worksheet is unnecessary.

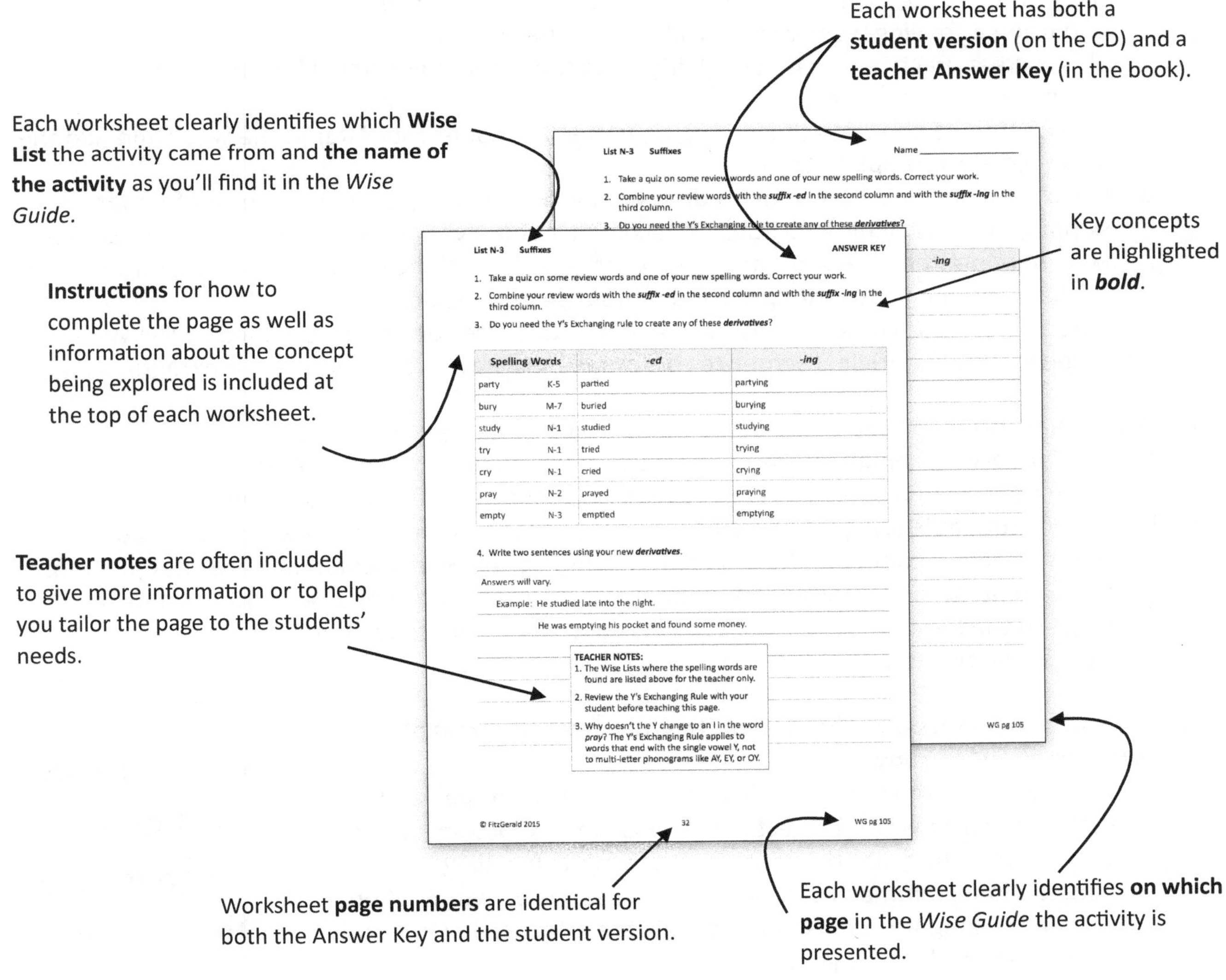

3. **Reference is to a single, male student** for ease and clarity in writing. It is clearly understood that students can also be female and that a teacher might be working with a group or a class.

4. **Multiple possibilities for student answers** are often listed on the Teacher Answer Keys.
   a. These are not always an exhaustive list. You may find more options. Let us know when you do! http://www.swrtraining.com/contact-us/
   b. Usually the student is only required to come up with one answer, unless multiple options are requested in the instructions.

5. **Worksheet Instructions are written to the student.**
   a. Help him read the instructions until he can do so himself.
   b. Your teaching instructions can be found in this area.

It is critical that you have your student writing as much as possible.

6. **Writing assignments are often included as an added reinforcement**.
   a. Children master their spelling as they continue to be exposed to new words and especially in the context of sentences. They need regular practice with sentence writing.
   b. Many of the assignments ask the student to write a sentence or two using a spelling word or a derivative that they just created. This is great practice that helps solidify what they're learning and which provides you with an on-the-spot grammar lesson.
   c. Low on time? Either skip the writing or, better yet, come back later in the week and add the sentence(s) to complete the page.
   d. It is critical that you have your student writing as much as possible, so be careful that skipping these assignments doesn't become a habit. I've watched over and over as students who were omitting the sentence writing struggled...until they started including this. Both the student's reading and writing started to flourish as a result.
   e. These writing assignments may be in addition to those specifically outlined in *The Wise Guide* for writing original sentences or for taking dictation on sentences or paragraphs.

7. **Worksheets provide "Extra" pages for Primary Learning Log users.**
   a. The Primary Learning Log does not have Reference Pages for some of the rules. The worksheets now provide a way to cover these concepts when necessary in Lists N and O.
   b. If your student is using the Black Learning Log, use the Reference Pages in your student's Learning Log to complete the assignment and skip the worksheets; they are intended more for students who are using the Primary Log. However, when you use up your Reference Pages in the Log, you have a backup place and/or activity to continue working on the concept.

8. **The assignments require the student to write from his brain as much as possible, not to copy**.
   a. Your goal is for the student to instantly know how to spell and, therefore, write words correctly when his brain is focusing on the *content* of writing, not the *mechanics* of writing (spelling, punctuation, grammar, etc.). Copying is a passive activity that does not lead to long-term mastery. Dynamic brain-focused activities are vital to accomplish this goal.

Copying is a passive activity that does not lead to long-term mastery.

b. These worksheets occasionally include assignments for which the student is to hunt for words in his Learning Log. In this case, his log is a resource for finding more words that fit a concept he's working on.

II. LESSON PLANNING

1. **FIRST, start with the Wise Guide** and read through the suggested activities for the list(s) you're teaching.
   a. Select which activities are appropriate for your student based on
      1) where he is in the Wise List
      2) whether he's a reader
      3) how much writing he can do
      4) whether he's been through the list(s) before
      5) interest and need
   b. He does NOT need to complete every activity for each list each year. Ideally he'll repeat lists and can pick up other activities the second time through (see SWR p. 64).

2. **THEN look for whether there is a worksheet.**
   a. Remember, not all the activities lend themselves to a worksheet, so if you only go by what's in the worksheets, you'll miss some great activities!
   b. There are a few extra pages in the worksheets that you won't find assignments for in *The Wise Guide*. They are marked "Extra" on the Table of Contents and on the lower right corner of these worksheets since there is no corresponding Wise Guide page.

3. **Integrate your lessons to save on time!**
   a. The majority of worksheets start with a quiz. Use this as a followup to new words you just taught (see SWR p. 90, 4.).
   b. Quizzes are an excellent way to reinforce new material, and you have just set up a language activity to complete either now or later in the week — two activities in one!
   c. Schedule the worksheet quiz for when you have just taught the last of that week's list. It is common for an entire list to have been taught in order to use a reinforcement activity.

4. **Immediately correct work** - don't let your student practice errors.
   a. Before moving into the meat of the activity, be sure your student has spelled everything correctly from the quiz.
   b. Have him make the corrections on the page rather than your writing them for him. Re-writing is a valuable part of the learning experience for him. Have him say the phonogram sounds while he writes them.

> Immediately correct his work. Don't let him practice his errors.

5. **Modify requirements as necessary.**
   a. The worksheets are meant to be a help to you, not dictate how your lessons will necessarily play out.
   b. For example, an assignment may include creating derivatives for all 20 spelling words. You might modify that to require only 10 or 15, if that is more appropriate to your student.

c. Sentence writing goals can always be adjusted, and some assignments even include a blank at the top of the page in the student's instructions for you to fill in the number of sentences you're requiring of your student.

6. **Use flash cards to teach word-building activities.**
   a. Make a copy of WG pp. 98 and 116 for suffix and prefix cards. Cut these apart and tuck them away in an envelope for activities in which your student is creating derivatives.
   b. Build a set of flash cards as you work your way through *The Wise Guide* and keep them organized so you can quickly pull out the cards you need for review words. I used a shoe box and made dividers for the alphabet.
   c. As adults, we understand the process for mentally mixing and rearranging language components, but young ones are ***concrete learners***, which means they benefit from physically manipulating the language to understand how we can mix and match or rearrange word parts to create new words.
   d. Once older students understand how to mentally mix and match words and word parts, these flash cards aren't as necessary. However, some students will need them all the time.

7. **Have students practice reading their work, especially sentences.**
   a. The student's Learning Log and these activities make up his first "reader" (see SWR p. 120).
   b. Have him find people he can read his writing to. This strengthens his reading skills and builds excitement for future writing. Writers need an audience!

III. INDEPENDENT WORK vs. GUIDED LEARNING

> The moment you ask the student to complete an assignment independently, it has become a test of what he knows — or doesn't know.

1. When the idea of a worksheet comes to mind, **most teachers think "independent work."**
   a. Regardless of the extent of your instruction on a concept, the moment you ask the student to complete an assignment independently, it has become a "test" of what he knows — or doesn't know — rather than a continuation of your teaching.
   b. You have a lost teaching opportunity when the student makes multiple errors on a worksheet and then just moves on to the next activity. Yes, you can check off that assignment as "completed" and assign a poor grade, but the student either learned next to nothing or will remember incorrect information.
   c. Only use the worksheet as an independent activity if he can do so successfully on his own. That means that completing the worksheet together may be part of your lesson plan.

2. **Teaching vocabulary is a huge part of teaching reading**.
   a. As children grow and mature, their vocabulary needs to develop as well.
   b. A good vocabulary is necessary for strong reading comprehension. A child can have good decoding skills, but if he doesn't know what the words mean, he won't understand what he's reading.
   c. Many of the activities are intended to teach and stretch the student's vocabulary.

d. Teachers may find their own vocabulary being stretched. Model for your students a love for learning and get comfortable saying, "Let's look it up!" You're not expected to know it all, and your students will benefit greatly from your example of being willing to learn and grow.
e. This is especially important for teachers who have learned English as a second language. Plan to learn along with your student.

A good vocabulary is necessary for strong reading comprehension.

3. **Students will need your help** determining if a word they're building is a legitimate English word.
   a. During compound word activities, kids will commonly select common two-word phrases or hyphenated words, which are not real compound words. For example: *makeup* is a compound word but *made up* is a common two-word phrase that includes a verb & preposition.
   b. When adding prefixes or suffixes to base words, kids get the idea of mixing and matching but don't necessarily make legitimate words.
   c. Use a good dictionary or an online resource such as http://dictionary.reference.com or http://www.thefreedictionary.com. Mobile apps are helpful with common words but are often insufficient for the kind of word study you want to do, especially in the later Wise Lists.

IV. An ERRATA Page will be listed on our web site. Let us know if you find something that you think is a typographical error. We'll check it out and add it to the list for others' benefit.

http://www.swrtraining.com/enrichment-activity-worksheets-errata/

Wise Guide
Enrichment Activity
Worksheets

For Multiple Lists

Date:	Score:
1.	
2.	
3.	
4.	
5.	
6.	
7.	
8.	
9.	
10.	

Date:	Score:
1.	
2.	

Teacher Notes:

1. At the beginning of each day's lesson, the student needs to take a phonogram quiz (see SWR Step #5 & #6, p. 40).
2. Use one of these pages each week and write the Wise List(s) you're currently studying at the top so you can keep track of where the student was during this time.
3. Encourage daily quizzes, rather than quizzing four times on one day.
4. Select phonograms that will be included in that day's dictation, phonograms that need review, or new phonograms the student has recently learned.
5. You can also use this warmup quiz to review words missed on previous spelling tests.
6. Limit your quizzes to 5-10 items each day. Consistent and quick quizzes are an effective way to review these invaluable phonograms.

Date:	
1.	
2.	
3.	
4.	
5.	
6.	
7.	
8.	
9.	
10.	

	Score:
3.	
4.	
5.	
6.	
7.	
8.	
9.	
10.	

Time for reading 70 phonograms: _________ seconds

Date:	Score:
1.	
2.	
3.	
4.	
5.	
6.	
7.	
8.	
9.	
10.	

Date:	Score:
1.	
2.	

Teacher Notes:

1. As early as List I-4, you can start timing the student once a week while he reads the phonograms with just their sounds, not the rules or any other phonogram language. For example, for the AY phonogram, he would merely say the sound /A/, not the whole dialogue like he normally does ("AY, the two-letter /A/, that we MAY use at the end of English words").
2. At the beginning of each day's lesson, the student needs to take a phonogram quiz (see SWR Step #5 & #6, p. 40).
3. Use one of these pages each week and write the Wise List(s) you're currently studying at the top so you can keep track of where the student was during this time.
4. Encourage daily quizzes, rather than quizzing four times on one day.
5. Select phonograms that will be included in that day's dictation, phonograms that need review, or new phonograms the student has recently learned.
6. You can also use this warmup quiz to review words missed on previous spelling tests.
7. Limit your quizzes to 5-10 items each day. Consistent and quick quizzes are an effective way to review these invaluable phonograms.

Date:	
1.	
2.	
3.	
4.	
5.	
6.	
7.	
8.	
9.	
10.	

	Score:
9.	
10.	

70 Phonogram Quiz Score ______/______ **ANSWER KEY**

Date ______________________

1		30		59	
2		31		60	
3		32		61	
4		33		62	
5		34		63	
6		35		64	
7		36		65	
8		37		66	
9					
10					
11					
12					
13					
14					
15					
16					
17					
18					
19					
20					
21		50			
22		51			
23		52			
24		53			
25		54			
26		55			
27		56			
28		57			
29		58			

Teacher Notes:

1. Periodically, you'll want to give your student a quiz on all the phonograms he has learned. Give this quiz at the end of each school quarter for a good assessment of student progress.
2. Print out an extra copy of the student page for this worksheet and label it "Answer Key." Write in the phonograms in the order you're going to dictate them so that you have an answer key that matches that specific quiz. Vary the order of phonograms on each quiz you give.
3. To indicate your student's score, enter the total correct out of how many phonograms you gave on the quiz. For example: 63/70 would mean the student wrote 63 phonograms correctly out of 70 administered.

70 Phonogram Plus Quiz Score ______/______ **ANSWER KEY**

Date ____________________

1		30		59	
2		31		60	
3		32		61	
4		33		62	
5					
6					
7					
8					
9					
10					
11					
12					
13					
14					
15					
16					
17					
18					
19					
20					
21					
22					
23					
24					
25		54		83	
26		55		84	
27		56		85	
28		57		86	
29		58		87	

Teacher Notes:

1. Periodically, you'll want to give your student a quiz on all the phonograms he has learned. Give this quiz at the end of each school quarter for a good assessment of student progress.
2. Print out an extra copy of the student page for this worksheet and label it "Answer Key." Write in the phonograms in the order you're going to dictate them so that you have an answer key that matches that specific quiz. Vary the order of phonograms on each quiz you give.
3. To indicate your student's score, enter the total correct out of how many phonograms you gave on the quiz. For example: 57/74 would mean the student wrote 57 phonograms correctly out of 74 administered (70 basic + 4 advanced phonograms).
4. Once your student has started learning advanced phonograms (SWR Step #38), you can include them on the quiz (see spaces #71-87). Whether you include these phonograms for a grade or just for practice is up to you. However, if you're going to include advanced phonograms on this quiz, be sure you're quizzing them frequently on your daily phonogram quizzes as preparation.
5. Advanced phonogram cards are not required but are helpful for more frequent review once an advanced phonogram has been introduced. See our web site for these cards. www.swrtraining.com

1. Look at the ***Silent Final E Reference Page*** in your Learning Log and use it to complete this page.
2. Add the ***silent final E*** markings to all of the words listed below.
3. Any other markings have already been done for you.

Teacher Note:
Use this page after teaching the Silent Final E's to reinforce the new rules. This page works best with students who have some reading ability.

cake	glue 2	hinge 3
these (2, 2)	tone	charge 3
dance 3	serve 2	house 5
carve 2	ap ple 4	style
type	tape	pad dle 4
tense 5	fine	val ue 2
gig gle 4	goose 5	splurge 3

Write & Draw

Teacher Notes:

1. At least once weekly you want your student to be writing sentences or some other directed writing activity.
2. Use this page with a young student who is making progress on his penmanship, as the lines are closer in size to those found in the Learning Log.
3. The sentences do not need to be related.
4. Encourage him to choose one of his sentences to illustrate in the space above.

1. Take a quiz on 27 phonograms. Write them in any box you like to mix it up.
2. As your teacher calls out a phonogram, find it and cross it out. Draw a line through every three phonograms that you cross out in a row. Cross out a box when you have all of the phonograms inside it crossed out. When you have all three boxes crossed out, you've got a THREENGO!

Teacher Notes:

1. Make copies of this page to pull out when you need a fun change of pace for phonogram or review word review.
2. Include phonograms from a new spelling list you're teaching that day so they're fresh, and the student is ready to use them in new words.
3. For efficient paper usage, put this page in a sheet protector or one of the Quick Response sleeves found at www.swrtraining.com. The student uses a dry erase marker and then simply wipes it clean when he's done.

1. Take a quiz on 25 phonograms. Write them in any of the pathway steps you like.
2. When you use a phonogram in your spelling words, cross it out.
3. Once you have crossed out all of your pathway steps, you can move from START to FINISH!

START

Teacher Notes:

1. Make copies of this page to pull out when you need a fun change of pace for phonogram or review word review.
2. Include phonograms from a new spelling list you're teaching that day so they're fresh, and the student is ready to use them in new words.
3. After you teach each new spelling word, have the student cross out any of the phonograms used in that word that he wrote on this page.
4. For efficient paper usage, put this page in a sheet protector or one of the Quick Response sleeves found at www.swrtraining.com. The student uses a dry erase marker and then simply wipes it clean when he's done.

FINISH

1. Take a quiz on 24 spelling words and/or phonograms. Write them in any box you like to mix it up.
2. Correct them to be sure everything is written correctly.
3. As your teacher calls out the words and/or phonograms, cross them out. You can call out "BINGO" every time you get five in a row. Keep going until all your boxes are crossed out.

Teacher Notes:

1. Make copies of this page to pull out when you need a fun change of pace for phonogram or review word review.
2. Include phonograms from a new spelling list you're teaching that day so they're fresh, and the student is ready to use them in new words.
3. For efficient paper usage, put this page in a sheet protector or one of the Quick Response sleeves found at www.swrtraining.com. The student uses a dry erase marker and then simply wipes it clean when he's done.

		FREE ★ **SPOT**		

Wise Guide
Enrichment Activity
Worksheets

Lists N-1 to N-8

1. Write your review spelling words below as your teacher dictates them.
2. Practice using these words in your writing so that you can spell them quickly and correctly.

Teacher Notes:

1. Incorporated into the lesson plans for Wise Lists M & N are activities for reviewing Lists A-I. These early lists include over 50% of the words we read and write, so long-term mastery of them is important!
2. Each Wise List has a two-page spread. Look for the "Review Words from A-I" activities that are listed at the top of the right-hand page for Lists N-1 through N-8.
3. You'll give a quick quiz on those words, which could be on lined paper or on one of the "Review Words" Worksheets included in this book. This helps you do the review quiz AND get a new language arts activity started.
4. Any words the student misses on the quiz will then be dictated with full spelling dictation (see SWR pp. 69-76) onto copies you make of this page. You'll recognize the format is similar to the Primary Learning Log, with room for parts of letters to go below the baseline without interfering with the word below it.
5. Each week, have your student add any new review words to this page and keep it in his Language Arts binder to study. You can add to it each time you teach new review words. These words should show up on the end-of-the week tests and on daily warm-up quizzes.
6. For more information on this valuable review, see WG p. 83.

1. Write your review spelling words below as your teacher dictates them.
2. Practice using these words in your writing so that you can spell them quickly and correctly.

Teacher Notes:

1. Incorporated into the lesson plans for Wise Lists M & N are activities for reviewing Lists A-I. These early lists include over 50% of the words we read and write, so long-term mastery of them is important!
2. Each Wise List has a two-page spread. Look for the "Review Words from A-I" activities that are listed at the top of the right-hand page for Lists N-1 through N-8.
3. You'll give a quick quiz on those words, which could be on lined paper or on one of the "Review Words" Worksheets included in this book. This helps you do the review quiz AND get a new language arts activity started.
4. Any words the student misses on the quiz will then be dictated with full spelling dictation (see SWR pp. 69-76) onto copies you make of this page. You'll recognize the format is similar to the Black Learning Log, so have your student skip the shaded lines.
5. Each week, have your student add any new review words to this page and keep it in his Language Arts binder to study. You can add to it each time you teach new review words. These words should show up on the end-of-the week tests and on daily warm-up quizzes.
6. For more information on this valuable review, see WG p. 83.

1. Take a quiz on three ***compound words*** from List N-1, some review words, and some of your new spelling words. Correct your work.
2. Combine your spelling words with the review words to create one ***compound word*** for each spelling word. You might need to add a ***suffix*** to make a real English word.

Compound Words		
himself	itself	something

Review Words				
about	baby	fire	out	road
after	bow	in	over	under
at	by	less	payer	with

Spelling Words	Compound Words
study	outstudy, overstudy, understudy
try	tryout (as a noun; "to try out" as a verb is two words)
write	overwrite, underwrite
hear	outhear, overhear
balance	overbalance
cry	outcry, crybaby
act	overact
use	useless, overuse, underuse
tax	overtax, taxpayer
thought	afterthought, thoughtless
size	oversized, undersized
rule	overrule
number	outnumber, numberless
there	thereabout, thereat, thereby, therein, therewith
cross	crossfire, crossover, crossbow, crossroad

Teacher Note: While multiple possibilities are listed, the student only needs to write one compound word for each spelling word.

Combine your ***prefixes*** and ***suffixes*** with the base word ***act*** to form as many ***derivatives*** as you can.

act *derivatives*		

Teacher Notes:

1. Use the *suffix* and *prefix* cards from WG pp. 98 and 116 with a 3x5 card for *act.*
2. See the *Alpha List* p. 72 and SWR pp. 130-131 for more on *derivatives* that can be formed from the base word *act.* There are 85 possibilities while this page allows for 36 answers.

1. Take a quiz on some of your review words and two of your new spelling words. All of these words can be used as ***prepositions***.
2. Correct your quiz so that everything is spelled correctly.
3. Write ________ sentences, using at least one ***preposition*** from your list in each one. When you use the ***preposition*** with a ***noun*** (*on a table, under the bed, with six cats*) or ***pronoun*** (*to her, at them, with us*), you are creating a ***prepositional phrase***.
4. Circle your ***prepositions*** and underline the entire ***prepositional phrase***.

Prepositions				
about	at	for	on	up
after	beyond	in	out	under
among	by	into	over	with
	down	of	to	

Teacher Notes:
1. Determine how many sentences you would like your student to write and fill that number in the blank for #3.
2. See p. 23 of this book for more information on *prepositional phrases*.

1. ***Prepositions*** are words that explain a relationship between two things.

   *The book is **on** the nice table.*

   The sentence above tells us how the book and the table are related (*on*).

2. A ***prepositional phrase*** includes a ***preposition***, a ***noun*** or a ***pronoun***, and any ***adjectives*** describing the ***noun*** or ***pronoun***.

3. We can build better sentences when we understand the role of each part of speech in a sentence and how they relate to one another. Diagramming sentences helps us do just that.

4. Connected lines show how our words (part of speech) relate to one another. The example below shows the diagram for the ***prepositional phrase*** in the example sentence above.
   a. We connect the ***preposition*** and ***noun/pronoun*** lines to show that they are related.
   b. The ***adjectives*** lines are connected to the ***noun/pronoun*** line they describe.

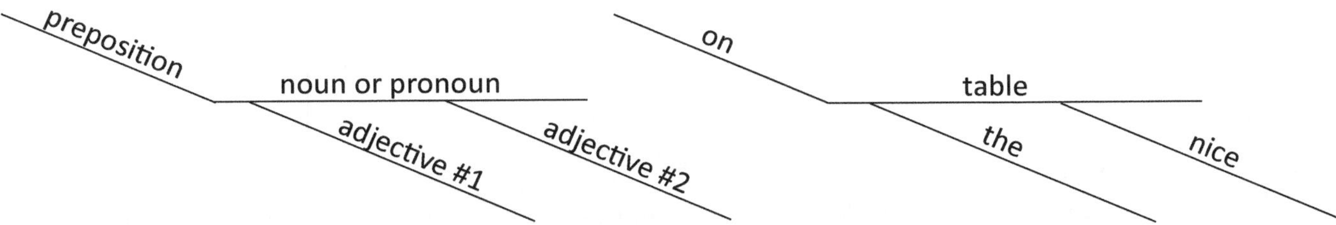

5. On separate paper, write four sentences using ***prepositions*** from List N-1. Remember, to be a true ***prepositional phrase*** it must have a ***preposition*** and a ***noun*** or ***pronoun***.

6. Diagram below the ***prepositional phrases*** you used in your sentences. Fill in any adjectives that you used as well.

Teacher Notes:

1. A *prepositional phrase* includes the *preposition* (P) and the *noun* (N) or *pronoun* (PN) that follows it. Example: to (P) Peter (N) for (P) him (PN)
2. A *prepositional phrase* might include an entire *noun phrase* (NP), which includes the *noun* and any words that describe it.
   Example: to (P) the busy store (NP) for (P) my wonderful mother (NP)
3. For this assignment, the student needs to diagram the entire *prepositional phrase*.
4. The word *to* is a *preposition* when it is followed by a *noun, a noun phrase, or a pronoun.* However, it is part of a *verb phrase* when it is followed by a *verb.*

Prepositional Phrases	Verb Phrases
to the store	to go
to her mom	to eat
to him	to have

1. When we write, our sentences can tend to follow the simple pattern of ***Subject/Verb***. If we use this pattern over and over and over and over, it can become a bit boring for the reader.
2. One of the ways we can make our writing better is to change the way we start our sentences.
3. Instead of a ***subject***, we could start our sentences with a ***prepositional phrase***, which includes a ***preposition***, a ***noun*** or ***pronoun***, and any ***adjectives*** describing the noun.

   Under the bed hid the cat. *Out of the hat jumped a white rabbit.*
4. If our ***prepositional phrase*** is a little long, we add a ***comma*** before beginning the rest of the sentence.

   After a prepositional phrase, he needs to have a noun.
   Beyond the lovely blue skies, I want to fly one day.
5. Write ________ sentences, using a ***prepositional phrase*** at the beginning of each one.
6. (Circle) your ***prepositions*** and <u>underline</u> the entire ***prepositional phrase***.

Teacher Notes:

1. Write in the number for how many sentences you want your student to write.
2. To help your student write sentences that start with a *prepositional phrase:*
   a. Make a list of *prepositions* on the board or have him look at page B30 in his Black Learning Log (*Prepositions* page). See SWR p. 104 for a list.
   b. Have him orally tell you a sentence using one of these *prepositions* and one or more of his List N-1 words. For example: I will study before the test.
   c. Write his sentence on the board.
   d. Have him identify the *prepositional phrase* (before the test).
   e. Rewrite the sentence with that phrase at the beginning of the sentence (Before the test I will study.)
   f. Have him read the new sentence.
   g. Erase the board and have him write his sentence.
3. Sometimes a sentence starting with a *prepositional phrase* sounds a bit awkward. That's normal because we don't always talk like this and because some of these sentences sound better than others. That's okay. Your student is practicing a new writing skill. First he has to learn how to write with this new sentence structure and then practice it. Once he gets better at it, he will use this opener more sparingly and more naturally.

1. Take a quiz on some review words and some of your new spelling words. Correct your work.
2. Combine your review words with the ***suffix -ing***. Do you need the E's Dropping rule?
3. Combine your spelling words with the ***suffixes*** listed below to create one ***derivative*** for each spelling word. Do you need to use the E's Dropping or Y's Exchanging rules?

Review Words	*-ing*
cry	crying
study	studying
tax	taxing
act	acting

Review Words	*-ing*
cross	crossing
try	trying
size	sizing
write	writing

TEACHER NOTE: Dictate the words in **bold** on this page. Your student will create the derivatives for the upper and lower charts.

Suffixes				
-able	*-ate*	*-er*	*-hood*	*-ly*
-ance	*-ed*	*-ess*	*-ic*	*-ory*

TEACHER NOTE: Multiple options are shown below, but the student only needs to write one derivative for each spelling word.

Spelling Words	Derivatives
person	personable
press	pressed
guide	guidance, guided
doctor	doctored, doctorate
teacher	teacherly
priest	priestess, priesthood, priestly
woman	womanhood, womanly
village	villager
angel	angelic
demand	demanded

Spelling Words	Derivatives
excuse	excusable, excused
offer	offertory, offered
question	questionable, questioned
pray	prayed
confess	confessed
mumble	mumbled, mumbler
repent	repented
criticize	criticized
reason	reasonable, reasoned

1. In the first column, take a quiz on some of your spelling words. Correct your work.
2. The words you wrote are ***action verbs,*** meaning that they describe ***actions*** or ***what someone does***.
3. ***Verbs*** also tell us ***when*** something happens, happened, or will happen. This is called ***tense.*** The ***verbs*** you wrote are in ***present tense***, meaning it is something that happens regularly.

   I *sleep* at night. I *eat* my dinner. I *play* outside.

4. Practice adding the ***ED ending*** to your ***verbs*** to make them ***past tense***. Write the new word in the correct column, depending on the sound the ***ED phonogram*** is saying.

Present Tense	ed	ed (2)	ed (3)
press			pressed
guide	guided		
doctor		doctored	
demand	demanded		
excuse		excused	
offer		offered	
question		questioned	
pray		prayed	
confess			confessed
mumble		mumbled	
repent	repented		
reason		reasoned	

TEACHER NOTES:
1. Use this page if your student is using the Primary Learning Log.
2. Black Log users could add these words to B19 & B20 instead of using this worksheet.

5. Write a sentence using one of your new ***past tense verbs***.

Answers will vary.

Example: He offered his excuses.

The teacher questioned the children.

1. Take a quiz on your review spelling words below.
2. Correct your words to be sure everything is spelled correctly.
3. These are words that are more expressive or more precise ways of describing a ***person*** or how someone ***says*** something. They help the reader understand more clearly what a writer is trying to communicate.
4. Add a check mark in the column to indicate whether it's another word for ***a person*** or for ***to say***.

Spelling Words	Person	Say
ask		✓
beg		✓
boy	✓	
call		✓
child	✓	
loner	✓	
lord	✓	
mother	✓	
page		✓
read		✓
sang		✓
tell		✓
thank		✓

5. Write a sentence using one of these more ***vivid words*** from each column.

Answers will vary.

Example: The child begged for a treat.

His mother sang her baby to sleep.

1. ***Quotation marks*** are used at the beginning and at the end of the exact words someone has said.

   "May I have one?" asked the doctor.

2. A ***comma*** is used at the end of a ***sentence tag*** when we introduce a ***quote***.

   The teacher asked, "Is that yours?"

3. A ***capital letter*** is used at the beginning of every ***quoted sentence.*** The ***end mark*** of the last sentence of the ***quote*** is inside the ***closing quotation marks***.

4. Write ________ sentences using your List N spelling words and including a direct quote in each.

5. Use the correct punctuation such as capital letters, periods, commas, and at least two quotes with ***quotation marks***.

Teacher Notes:

1. Determine how many sentences you would like your student to write and fill that number in the blank for #4.
2. See WG p. 103 for more on this activity and SWR Step #23 for instructions on teaching writing.
3. Putting ideas, words, correct spelling, proper grammar, *and* punctuation together is a *lot* to remember for a young student. In the beginning when the student writes independently, much of the punctuation will be caught in the editing process.

1. Good writers use ***vivid words***. These are words that are more expressive or more precise. They help the reader understand more clearly what the writer is trying to communicate.
2. Take a quiz on your new spelling words below. Write the words that refer to ***people*** or ***people groups*** in the first column.
3. In the second column write in ***past tense*** the words that refer to how people ***say*** something. Will you need to use the E's Dropping rule to add the ***ED ending***?
4. Correct your words to be sure everything is spelled correctly.

Persons	Say
person	demanded
press	excused
guide	offered
doctor	questioned
teacher	prayed
priest	confessed
woman	mumbled
women	repeated
village	criticized
angel	reasoned

Teacher Notes:
1. Dictate the words in pairs ***as they occur in the Learning Log*** (*person-demand*, *press-excuse*, etc.).
2. Dictate the *verbs* ("say" column) ***as present tense***, just as they are in the Learning Log. It's the student's job to change each *verb* into its *past-tense* version.

5. Write a sentence using one of these more ***vivid words*** from each column.

Answers will vary.

Example: The guide questioned the guests.

The angel offered the woman a promise.

1. Take a quiz on some review words. Correct your work to be sure everything is spelled correctly.

Review Words			
a	each	low	that
an	ice	odd	thick
the	just	other	west
all	late	soft	wild
brave	long	spring	winter

2. Each of the words you wrote can be used as an ***adjective,*** a word that is used to describe a ***noun.***
3. Look through your Learning Log for words in List N that are ***nouns*** that these ***adjectives*** could describe. Write ***adjective-noun combinations*** below for each of your review words.
4. Make sure your ***adjectives*** and ***nouns*** match in number.

Teacher Notes:

1. The student only needs to write two-word combinations here.
   Examples: *a pearl*
   all categories
   each bulletin
   spring sky
2. Note that the *noun* needs to match the *adjective* in number (e.g. *a category* vs. *all categories*).
3. Is your student able to identify the nouns in his Learning Log? Remind him that *nouns* name *persons, places, things,* or *ideas.*
4. As needed, help him brainstorm different *adjective-noun combinations.*
5. Modify this assignment to require fewer combinations.
6. Follow up on this assignment with the Adjectives Sentences worksheet on p. 31.

1. Look over your ***adjective-noun*** combinations that you wrote on the Review Words from A-I — Adjectives worksheet.

2. Write ________ sentences, using these ***adjective-noun*** combinations.

3. Underline your ***adjective-noun*** combinations.

Teacher Notes:

1. Determine how many sentences you would like your student to write and fill that number in the blank for #2.

2. If your student tends to write simple or short sentences, consider having him to add a *prepositional phrase* to each sentence (see p. 23 of this book).

1. Take a quiz on some review words and one of your new spelling words. Correct your work.
2. Combine your review words with the ***suffix -ed*** in the second column and with the ***suffix -ing*** in the third column.
3. Do you need the Y's Exchanging Rule to create any of these ***derivatives***?

Spelling Words		*-ed*	*-ing*
party	K-5	partied	partying
bury	M-7	buried	burying
study	N-1	studied	studying
try	N-1	tried	trying
cry	N-1	cried	crying
pray	N-2	prayed	praying
empty	N-3	emptied	emptying

4. Write two sentences using your new ***derivatives***.

Answers will vary.

Example: He studied late into the night.

He was emptying his pocket and found some money.

TEACHER NOTES:
1. The Wise Lists where the spelling words are found are listed above for the teacher only.
2. Review the Y's Exchanging Rule with your student before teaching this page.
3. Why doesn't the Y change to an I in the word *pray*? The Y's Exchanging Rule applies to words that end with the single vowel Y, not to multi-letter phonograms like AY, EY, or OY.

1. Take a quiz on your new spelling words in the first column. Correct your work.
2. All of these words can be ***nouns*** so they can be ***plural,*** meaning "more than one."
3. Write your words again in the second column, changing them into the ***plural*** form. Are there any Y's Exchanging words?

Nouns	Plural Nouns
clap	claps
crystal	crystals
sky	skies
definition	definitions
need	needs
matter	matters
pearl	pearls
spirit	spirits
knee	knees
dollar	dollars
chicken	chickens
mistake	mistakes
category	categories
burial	burials
bulletin	bulletins
energy	energies
custom	customs
leather	leathers
empty	empties
oyster	oysters

1. Take a quiz on some review words in the first column. Correct your work.
2. Each of these words can be used as an ***action verb***.
3. In the second column, add the ***suffix -ing*** to each of these ***verbs***, and in the third column make each one ***past tense***.
4. Which of your words need the 1-1-1 Rule? Which of your ***past tense verbs*** are irregular?

Spelling Words	*-ing*	Past Tense
bag	bagging	bagged
belong	belonging	belonged
box	boxing	boxed
bow	bowing	bowed
bug	bugging	bugged
cover	covering	covered
gas	gassing	gassed
get	getting	**got**
hand	handing	handed
hit	hitting	**hit**
send	sending	**sent**
show	showing	showed
sin	sinning	sinned
star	starring	starred
tan	tanning	tanned
wash	washing	washed

Teacher Notes:

1. The irregular past tense verbs are shown in **bold** here for the teacher.
2. It is activities like this that reveal how your student's language learning is progressing. If he uses these *irregular* verbs correctly in his oral language, he is more likely to identify them as *irregular* in this activity. If he tries to add the *-ed suffix* to them, then repeatedly hearing them used correctly will help him use them correctly in both his oral and written language.

1. Take a quiz on your new spelling words in the first column. Correct your work.
2. In the next two columns, add the ***suffixes -ing*** and ***-ed*** to each of these words.
3. You'll need to use your spelling rules for some of these words. Which ones will you use?

E's Dropping 1-1-1 Y's Exchanging Just add ending

Spelling Words	*-ing*	*-ed*
curb	curbing	curbed
carry	carrying	carried
subject	subjecting	subjected
misspell	misspelling	misspelled
drug	drugging	drugged
erase	erasing	erased
fancy	fancying	fancied
hem	hemming	hemmed
dirty	dirtying	dirtied
hurry	hurrying	hurried
conquer	conquering	conquered
pare	paring	pared
plan	planning	planned
center	centering	centered
prove	proving	proved
copy	copying	copied
suffer	suffering	suffered
sign	signing	signed
market	marketing	marketed
voice	voicing	voiced

1. Good writers play with language to make it more interesting and fun for the reader.
2. One technique you can add to your writing is called ***alliteration,*** which is where a ***sound*** is repeated at the beginning of several words of a sentence. Read this sentence and listen for the ***sound*** that is repeated.

   The cat called for her kittens when they cried for milk.
3. As your teacher reads your spelling words, listen to the first ***sound*** of each word. Does it start with one of the ***sounds*** below? If so, write it under the appropriate ***sound***. (The letter inside the slashes indicates a ***sound***.)
4. Remember that different letters can spell the same sound. For example, both C and K can say the /k/ ***sound*** and C and S can both say the /s/ ***sound***.

/b/	/k/	/s/
burial	clap	sky
bulletin	crystal	spirit
bag	category	subject
belong	custom	center
box	curb	suffer
bow	carry	sign
bug	conquer	send
	copy	sin
	cover	star

Teacher Notes:

1. For your student's page to end up like this answer key, read the words ***as they appear in the WG in this order***:
   List N-3
   List N-4
   List N-4 Review words from A-I
2. Continue this activity with the *Alliteration* Sentences worksheet on p. 37.

1. Look at your ***Alliterations*** worksheet.
2. Use at least three of the words from the /b/ list to write a sentence. You're free to add more words to really saturate the sentence with your ***sounds***. (Did you hear that ***alliteration***?)
3. Repeat this process with each of the other lists from the worksheet. You'll have three ***alliteration*** sentences when you're done.
4. **BONUS**: Write two more ***alliteration*** sentences using other words from your Learning Log that start with the same ***sounds***.

Answers will vary.

Examples: The bag and the blue bug belonged with the bunny in the big box.

Can you conquer your custom clap in the crystal shop?

The star is in the center of the sky.

1. Take a quiz on some of your review words and one new spelling word. Correct your work.
2. In the second column, combine your ***helping verbs*** with a ***main verb*** from List N-5. You can also go back to Lists N-1 through N-4 to find more ***verbs***. Following are some examples.

   am crossing ***have*** studied ***are*** crying ***will*** practice

3. Make sure that your ***helping verbs*** match their ***main verb*** in ***number*** (single or plural), ***person*** (1st, 2nd, or 3rd), and ***tense*** (present, past, or future).

Helping Verbs	Helping Verb + Main Verb
am	**ANSWERS WILL VARY**
is	
are	
was	
were	
be	
have	
has	
had	
do	
did	
may	
might	
must	
should	
shall	
can	
could	
will	
would	
been	

Teacher Notes:

1. Dictate the Review Words from Lists A-I in the first column to your student. These can all be used as *helping verbs.*
2. The last word *been* is a new spelling word from List N-5.
3. Your student can use his Learning Log to find *main verbs* to combine with these *helping verbs* to make *verb phrases* in the second column.

1. ***Action verbs*** tell us what the ***subject*** of the sentence did. To be used correctly, they have to match the ***subject*** in certain ways, such as in ***person*** and ***number***.
2. Any ***helping verbs*** in the ***verb phrase*** must match the ***main verb*** in ***person***, ***number***, and ***tense***.
3. Take a quiz on three sentences. Finish each chart with the different versions of that sentence using the appropriate ***subject pronoun***.
4. Correct your work to be sure everything is spelled correctly and that your ***verbs*** match the ***subject*** and each other.

Person	
1st person	person speaking or writing
2nd person	person being spoken to
3rd person	person being spoken about

Number	
Singular	one
Plural	more than one

Tense	
Present	happening now or happens regularly
Past	before this moment
Future	has not yet happened

Person	**Singular**	**Plural**
Present Tense		
1st	I am captured.	We are captured.
2nd	You are captured.	You are captured.
3rd	**He is captured.**	They are captured.
Past Tense		
1st	I was exhausted.	We were exhausted.
2nd	You were exhausted.	You were exhausted.
3rd	**It was exhausted.**	They were exhausted.
Future Tense		
1st	I will inspect it.	We will inspect it.
2nd	You will inspect it.	You will inspect it.
3rd	**She will inspect it.**	They will inspect it.

Teacher Note: Dictate the sentences in **bold** to your student. He will complete the rest of them.

Teacher Note: If your student needs help with pronouns, see the Subject/Object Pronouns Introduction Worksheet on p. 40. For this Conjugation activity, you'll only be using Subject Pronouns.

1. Read these sentences. *Mother got something. Mother read a book. Listen to Mother. Do you hear Mother reading? Thank you, Mother.*

2. Saying "Mother" over and over and over can get tiring, so we use ***pronouns*** some of the time. Doesn't this sound better?

   Mother got something. She read a book. Listen to her.
   Do you hear her reading? Thank you, Mother.

3. Use the sample sentences to fill in the ***Pronoun*** chart below.

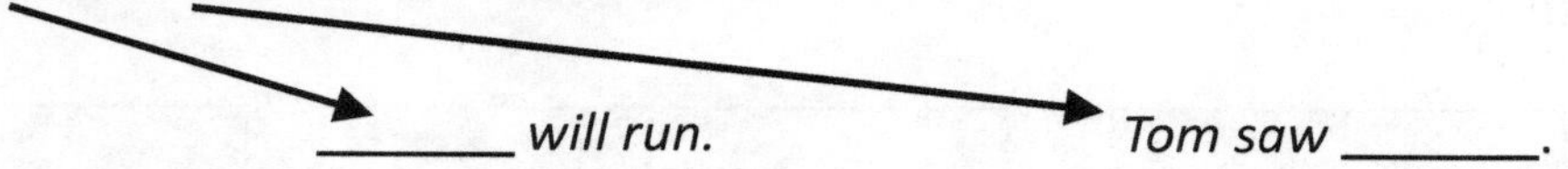

_______ will run. *Tom saw _______.*

Singular			
Person		**Subject**	**Object**
1st		I	me
2nd		you	you
3rd	M	he	him
	F	she	her
	N	it	it

Plural		
Person	**Subject**	**Object**
1st	we	us
2nd	you	you
3rd	they	them

Teacher Note: *Pronouns* tell us four things about the noun they're replacing.

a. **Person:** 1st person - person speaking
2nd person - person being spoken to
3rd person - person being spoken about

b. **Gender:** Masculine (males)
Feminine (females)
Neuter (neither one)
(Only 3rd person singular pronouns use gender.)

c. **Number:** singular (one)
plural (more than one)

d. **Case:** subject - person/thing doing the action
object - person/thing receiving the action

1. Take a quiz on some of your new spelling words in the ***Adjectives*** column.
2. Correct your work so that everything is spelled correctly.
3. Write each of your spelling words again as an ***adverb*** by adding the ***suffix -ly***.

Adjectives	Adverbs
cheerful	cheerfully
honest	honestly
fresh	freshly
rough	roughly
wise	wisely
wide	widely
plain	plainly
actual	actually
sure	surely
dependent	dependently
delightful	delightfully
faithful	faithfully

Teacher Note: When you add the *-ly suffix* to a word already ending with the letter L, you create a double consonant in the derivative. Does your student recognize this pattern?

4. Write two sentence using one of your new ***adverbs*** in each sentence.

Answers will vary.

Example: He wisely studied his spelling words.

She actually had to make her choice before noon.

1. An ***antonym*** is a word that means the ***opposite*** of something else. For example, *yesterday & tomorrow* or *exhaust & refresh* are antonyms.
2. Read the words in the first column. Which of your spelling words are the ***antonyms***? Write them in the second column.
3. Are there some left that you're not sure about? Listen as your teacher reads your spelling words to you. Write the last ones.

Antonyms	Spelling Words
fancy	plain
stale	fresh
foolish	wise
greatest	least
narrow	wide
expensive	cheap
dishonest	honest
uncertain	sure
old	young
grumpy	cheerful
grief	delight
smooth	rough
independent	dependent
never	always
past	future

1. An ***antonym*** is a word that means the opposite of something else. For example, *yesterday & today* or *capture & release* are ***antonyms***.
2. Take dictation on eight review words in the first column.
3. As your teacher dictates eight more review words, match them to their ***antonyms***.
4. Correct your work so that everything is spelled correctly.

Antonyms	
good	bad
yes	no
give	take
cold	hot
sick	well
big	little
gave	got
come	go

Teacher Notes:

1. Dictate the first column in the order listed here.
2. Dictate the second column ***in this order***:

   hot *well*
   little *no*
   bad *go*
   got *take*

3. You purposely want to dictate ***the second column in a scrambled order*** so that the student has to think carefully about the *antonyms* in order to match them.

5. Write a sentence using one of the ***antonyms*** listed above and then rewrite the sentence using the spelling word that means the ***opposite***. You'll have two sentences with ***opposite*** meanings when you're done. Underline the ***antonyms*** in each sentence.

Answers will vary.

Examples: The angel told the woman something good would happen.

The angel told the man something bad would happen.

1. Take a quiz on some of your new spelling words. Correct your work.
2. Create one ***derivative*** for each spelling word by combining your spelling words with the ***prefixes*** and ***suffixes*** listed below or combinations of each. One word will only match with another spelling word. Watch out for the E's Dropping words.

Prefixes			
dis-	*en-*	*other-*	*un-*
edge-	*in-*	*over-*	

Suffixes							
-age	*-en*	*-est*	*-ing*	*-ity*	*-ly*	*-ness*	*-ster*
-ed	*-er*	*-ful*	*-ist*	*-less*	*-ment*	*-s*	*-y*

Spelling Words	Derivatives
cheap	cheapen, cheapening, cheapened, cheaper, cheapest
cheerful	cheerfulness, cheerfully
honest	dishonesty, honestly
fresh	freshness, fresher, freshest, refresh, refreshed, refreshment
rough	roughage, roughen, roughness, rougher, roughest
wise	unwise, edgewise, wisely, otherwise, overwise, wiser, wisest
wide	wideness, widening, widened, wider, widest
plain	plainness, plains, plainer, plainest
actual	actuality, actually
sure	ensure, insure, surer, surest, surely
dependent	dependently, independent, independently
delight	delightful, delighting, delighted
future	futurist
choice	choicer, choicest
least	leastwise
young	younger, youngest, youngster
pair	pairing, paired, unpaired
faith	faithless, faithful
steal	stealing

Teacher Note: While multiple possibilities are listed, the student only needs to write one derivative for each spelling word.

Teacher Note: The word *leastwise* combines two spelling words from List N-6.

1. A ***synonym*** is a word that has a ***similar meaning*** as another word. For example, *rough* & *course* and *actual* & *definite* are ***synonyms***.
2. An ***associated*** word is one that relates in meaning or that is connected in some way with the idea of the other word. For example, *sink* & *swim* and *pen* & *ink* are ***associated*** words.
3. As your teacher dictates your spelling words, match it to its ***synonym*** or ***associated word(s)*** below.
4. Correct your work to be sure everything is spelled correctly.

Synonym or Associated Words	Spelling Words
underline	mark
reason	cause
low down	mean
burial	death
bow	arrow
love	court
equip totally	full
question	wonder
cross	bridge
curb	check
box	till
red	blood
show	fair
milk	dairy
letter	note
exhaust	tire
all but	except
in this way	thus
ahead	front
gas	smoke

1. As your teacher dictates some of your new spelling words, write them in the first column. These are ***verbs***. Two of your spelling words need to be turned into a ***verb*** so you can write it here.
2. Now write each word again as a ***past tense verb***. Watch out for the E's Dropping Rule.
3. Which phonogram sound or sounds did your ***ED ending*** make? Write the sound that the ***ED phonogram*** says in the word in the last column. If the verb was irregular and didn't use the ***ED ending***, write an X.

ed ***d*** ***t*** ***X***

4. Correct your work to be sure everything is spelled correctly.

Present Tense Verbs	Past Tense Verbs	ED Sound
mark	marked	t
bleed*	bled	X
front	fronted	ed
wonder	wondered	d
note	noted	ed
die*	died	d
cause	caused	d
bridge	bridged	d
court	courted	ed
fair	faired	d
smoke	smoked	t
tire	tired	d
mean	meant	X
check	checked	t
except	excepted	ed
till	tilled	d

Teacher Note: *The spelling words are *blood* and *death*, which are both nouns. Ask your student if he knows what the verb form of the word would be (*bleed* and *die*). Have him write these present tense verbs in the first column.

1. Take a quiz on some review words and on some of your new spelling words.
2. Correct your quiz so that everything is spelled correctly.
3. Combine your spelling words with the review words to create one ***compound word*** for each spelling word.

Review Words				
back	foot	land	shot	trade
bed	head	let	some	way
book	house	like	time	yard

Spelling Words	Compound Words
mark	bookmark, landmark, trademark
arrow	arrowhead
blood	bloodshot
front	frontlet
dairy	dairyland
note	footnote, notebook
death	deathbed, deathlike
cause	causeway
bridge	bridgehead, bridgeway
court	courthouse, courtyard, backcourt
fair	fairway
smoke	smokehouse
full	fullback
tire	tiresome
mean	meantime
check	checkbook

Teacher Note: While multiple possibilities are listed, the student only needs to write one compound word for each spelling word.

1. Word imagery adds a special dimension to writing. Consider these examples.

   The show was as dry as a bone. *You are the salt of the earth.*
   Her cheeks were like roses. *I am a worm.*

2. What do these sentences mean? A show cannot really be dry. A lady's cheeks don't really look like flowers. People aren't really salt. A person isn't really a worm.
3. These expressions are called ***similes*** and ***metaphors***, and they compare two things that aren't alike.

   simile uses ***as*** or ***like***

   metaphor says that one thing ***is*** the other

4. Good writers sprinkle these word pictures throughout their writing.
5. Write the ***similes*** and ***metaphors*** that your teacher dictates to you below.
6. Decide if what you wrote is a ***simile*** or a ***metaphor*** and (circle) the correct answer. Finally, underline your new spelling words.

simile
(metaphor) — A zipper of lightning opened a rain-filled sky.

(simile)
metaphor — The rowboats bobbed like bottle corks on the lake.

(simile)
metaphor — Stars seem like lamps set in the spacious Hall of the Creator.

Teacher Notes:
1. Teach these new words now, as necessary:
   bobbed (1-1-1 rule)
   lamps
   Hall
   Creator
2. Capitalize "Hall of the Creator" because it is being used as a title.
3. See WG p. 114 for the sources of these quotes.

1. A ***noun*** is a word for a person, a place, a thing, or an idea. An ***adjective*** is a word that describes a ***noun***.

   mother house bed love *red six the a*

2. Take a quiz on some review words and write them in the correct columns below, depending on whether the word is an ***adjective*** or a ***noun***.
3. Correct your work so that everything is spelled correctly.
4. On a separate page, write a sentence for each of these ***adjective-noun*** combinations.

Adjectives	Nouns
this	ring
free	toy
sick	baby
last	dance
best	doll
old	lace
nice	dinner
rich	men

Teacher Notes:

1. **Dictate these words together as pairs or two at a time.** For example you might say: "Write: *this ring.* Which is the *adjective* and which is the *noun*?"
2. Continue this activity with the Adjectives & Nouns Sentences worksheet on p. 50.

1. Write eight sentences using the ***adjective-noun*** pairs from your Review Words from A-I — Adjectives & Nouns worksheet. Use each of the ***four kinds of sentences*** twice.
2. Make sure each sentence is spelled correctly and that it begins and ends with the proper punctuation.

1. Answers will vary.

   Example: He will give her this ring.

   Mother made us a nice dinner.

Teacher Notes:

1. Students should write two of each sentence type (*declarative, interrogative, imperative, and exclamatory*).
2. See the Kinds of Sentences Worksheet, p. 51, for more on these sentence types.

2.

3.

4.

5.

6.

7.

8.

1. There are four basic ***kinds of sentences***.

   declarative sentences make statements
   interrogative sentences ask questions
   imperative sentences give commands
   exclamatory sentences express strong feeling

2. Write the sentences your teacher dictates to you, each as an example of the four ***sentence types***.
3. Be sure to use the correct end punctuation for each ***sentence type***.

State a fact.

We make rope of **hemp** and **flax**.

Ask a question?

How many **pints** make a quart?

Give a command.

Sue, iron the linen.

Show strong feeling!

It's poison!

Teacher Notes:
1. Teach the new words shown in **bold** now, if necessary:
   hemp
   flax
   pints
2. Optional: Use the student's name or someone you know instead of the name *Sue.*

. ? !

Wise Guide
Enrichment Activity
Worksheets

Lists O-1 to O-6

1. Sentences are complete ideas with two parts.

   The ***subject*** is who or what the sentence is about.
   The ***predicate*** includes a ***verb*** and tells something about the ***subject***.

Mother can read.	Who can read? What do we know about Mother?	**Mother** *(subject)* she **can read** *(predicate/verb)*
Father did sing.	Who sang? What do we know about Father?	**Father** *(subject)* he **did sing** *(predicate/verb)*

2. A ***verb phrase*** is made up of any ***helping verbs*** (*am, is*) and the ***verb*** in a sentence (*read, sing*).
3. Take a quiz on some review words that can be used as ***helping verbs.***

Helping Verbs			
can	did	shall	will
could	may	should	would

4. Take a quiz on some of your List O-1 spelling words.
   a. Write the words that are ***a subject*** (a person) in the first column.
   b. Select a ***helping verb*** to write with the ***verb*** (an action word) to form a ***verb phrase*** in the second column. You can only use a ***helping verb*** once.
5. Correct your quiz to be sure everything is spelled correctly.

Subject	Verb Phrase
sailor	***(helping verb will vary)*** request
nobody	***(helping verb will vary)*** object
police	***(helping verb will vary)*** address
thief	***(helping verb will vary)*** refuse
friend	***(helping verb will vary)*** mourn

Teacher Notes:

1. ***Dictate the word pairs together***.
   sailor - request
   nobody - object
   police - address
   thief - refuse
   friend - mourn
2. The student will write the *subject* word in the first column.
3. Then he will write one of the helping verbs and the *verb* in the second column.

1. Look at the words you wrote on the Subjects with Verb Phrases worksheet.
2. Write five simple sentences below by combining one of the ***subjects*** with any one of the ***verb phrases***.
3. Under the words, label your ***subject*** as ***S*** and underline your complete ***verb phrase***. See the examples below.

The teacher can speak.
S

A child did whisper.
S

Teacher Notes:

1. Can your student tell you who the sentence is about? That will be the *subject*. Have him label it with an S below the word.
2. Be sure that each of your student's sentences includes a *helping verb* from the Subjects with Verb Phrases worksheet on p. 54.
3. The *complete verb phrase* includes the *helping verb* **and** the main verb. Both are to be underlined.
4. Work through the first one with him. Is he able to do the next one on his own?

1.

2.

3.

4.

5.

1. ***Verbs*** tell us when something happens. This is called ***tense.***

Mary sings a song.	*present tense*	action is occurring now or is on-going
Mary sang a song.	*past tense*	action happened before now
Mary will sing a song.	*future tense*	action will happen at some time to come

2. ***Verbs*** match their ***subjects*** (who or what the sentence is about) in ***person***.

I sing.	I'm the one talking, so I'm the 1st person.
You sing.	I'm talking to you, so you're the 2nd person.
Tom sings.	We're talking about Tom, so he's the 3rd person.

3. When we use a ***verb*** to talk about a **3rd person**, we add *-s* or *-es* to the end of the ***verb*** so it matches our ***subject***.

1st or 2nd person	verb
3rd person	**verb + *-s*** or ***-es***

4. Take a quiz on your List O-1 spelling words.
   a. Write the words that are ***subjects*** (another name for a person) in the ***Subject*** column.
   b. Write the words that are ***verbs*** (action words) in the ***Verb*** column in **3rd person** (add ***-s*** or ***-es***).
5. Correct your quiz to be sure everything is spelled correctly.

Subject	Verb
author	indicates
aunt	repeats
uncle	explains
captain	sentences
chief	reproves
sailor	requests
nobody	objects
police	addresses
thief	refuses
friend	mourns

Teacher Notes:

1. Dictate these words ***in subject-verb pairs***, exactly ***as the words are listed in across from one another in your student's Learning Log***. For example, dictate:
   author indicate
   aunt repeat
   uncle explain
   etc.
2. Your student then selects which column to write each word in and the appropriate ending for the verb (adding *-s* or *-es*).

1. Look at the words you wrote on the Present Tense Verbs with Vivid Words worksheet.
2. Write five simple sentences below by combining one of the ***subjects*** with any one of the ***verbs*** using the ***present tense***. You will need to add ***-s*** or ***-es*** to the end of your ***verbs*** so the ***subject*** and ***verb*** match. Use each ***subject*** and ***verb*** only once.
3. Include a ***prepositional phrase*** in each sentence and underline it.
4. Under the words, label your ***subject*** (**S**) and your ***verb*** (**V**). See the examples below.

The teacher speaks to her class.
S V

A child whispers in church.
S V

Teacher Notes:

1. Your student will probably need to consult a list of prepositions to spark ideas for what to use in his sentences.
   - A student using the ***Primary Learning Log*** can refer to a list you write on the board (see SWR p. 104) or he can use Worksheets Book A-M p. 115.
   - A student using the ***Black Learning Log*** can consult p. B30 in his log.
2. Can he tell you ***who*** the sentence is about? That will be the *subject*, which he will label with an S.
3. What is the ***action word*** that he chose? That will be the *verb*, which he will label with a V.
4. Work through the first one with him. Is he able to do the rest on his own?

1.

2.

3.

4.

5.

1. Good writers use ***vivid words*** or words that are more expressive or more precise. They help the reader understand more clearly what the author is trying to communicate.
2. Take a quiz on your spelling words. These words include other words for a ***person*** and other words that describe how people ***speak*** to one another. Write the words in the correct column.
3. Correct your quiz to be sure everything is spelled correctly.

Person	Speaks
author	indicate
aunt	repeat
uncle	explain
captain	sentence
chief	reprove
sailor	request
nobody	object
police	address
thief	refuse
friend	mourn

Teacher Notes:

1. Dictate these words by ***alternating in a random order between the two columns***. For example, dictate: *author, aunt, indicate, repeat, uncle, explain, sentence, reprove, captain,* etc. Your student then selects in which column to write each word.
2. Dictate the verbs ***in the form they're listed in the WG***, not changing them to match the single subject. For example, dictate *indicate* **not** *indicates* even though *author indicates* is the correct verb usage. You'll work on subject/verb agreement on another assignment for List O-1.
3. Continue this assignment on the Present Tense Verbs with Vivid Words Sentences worksheet on p. 57.

1. Take a quiz on some review words and on some of your new spelling words. Correct your work.
2. Combine your spelling words with the review words to create one ***compound word*** for each spelling word.

Review Words					
air	hand	man	out	paper	teen*
band	land	moon	over	sale*	work

Teacher Note: There are two new words (*) included in this list. Help your student with these, if necessary.

Spelling Words	Compound Words
waste	wastepaper
ate	overate
hole	manhole
threw	overthrew
throw	overthrow
slide	landslide
struck	moonstruck
weather	weatherman
second	secondhand
weary	overweary
waist	waistband
eight	eighteen
whole	wholesale
through	throughout
needle	needlework
board	overboard
port	airport
station	outstation
rate	overrate
shine	outshine, moonshine

1. Take a quiz on some bonus review words and on some of your new spelling words.
2. Correct your work.
3. Combine your spelling words with the review words to create one ***compound word*** for each spelling word.

Bonus Review Words		
above	basket	key
away	birth	line
back	bill	sun
base	coat	way

Spelling Words	Compound Words
throw	throwaway, throwback
waste	wastebasket
hole	keyhole
slide	backslide
waist	waistcoat, waistline
through	throughway
board	aboveboard, baseboard, billboard, backboard
rate	birthrate
shine	sunshine

Teacher Note: Multiple options are listed, but the student only needs to create one compound word for each spelling word.

4. Write a sentence using one of your new ***compound words***.

Answers will vary.

Examples: His waistcoat looked smart under his jacket.

I enjoyed the sunshine when we went to the beach last summer.

1. Choose three pairs of homophones that you have learned so far. Write each word on a line below.
2. Illustrate your homophones.

TEACHER NOTE: Sample illustrations are shown below. The student may choose different words or to illustrate these words differently.

eight

ate

waste

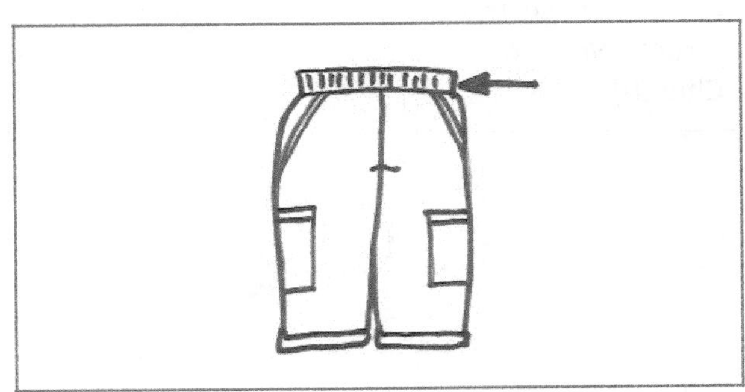

waist

whole

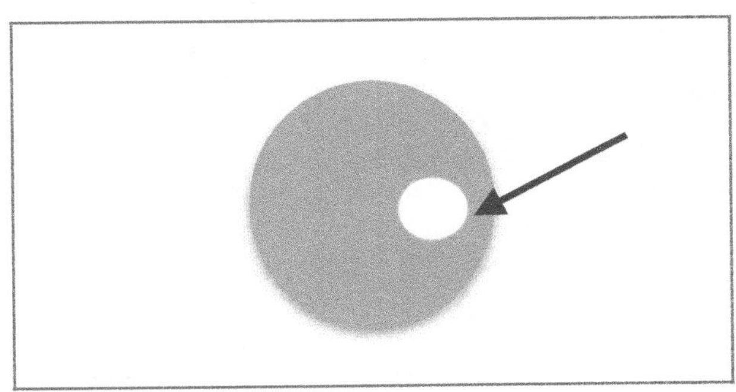

hole

1. What is the object that always points us in the direction of north? Write its name on the top line.
2. Label the object below with each of its four main points on the outside of the circle.
3. Add the abbreviations for each of the eight points inside the circle. Turn your page as you write.
4. At the bottom of the page, write the sentence your teacher dictates about this object.

Teacher Notes:

- Abbreviations for the compass points are capitalized (NW, SE, etc.).
- Names of the four directions (*north, south, east,* and *west*) are written with lower case letters.
- A direction word starts with a capital when it is part of a name (e.g. North First Street, West End Church).

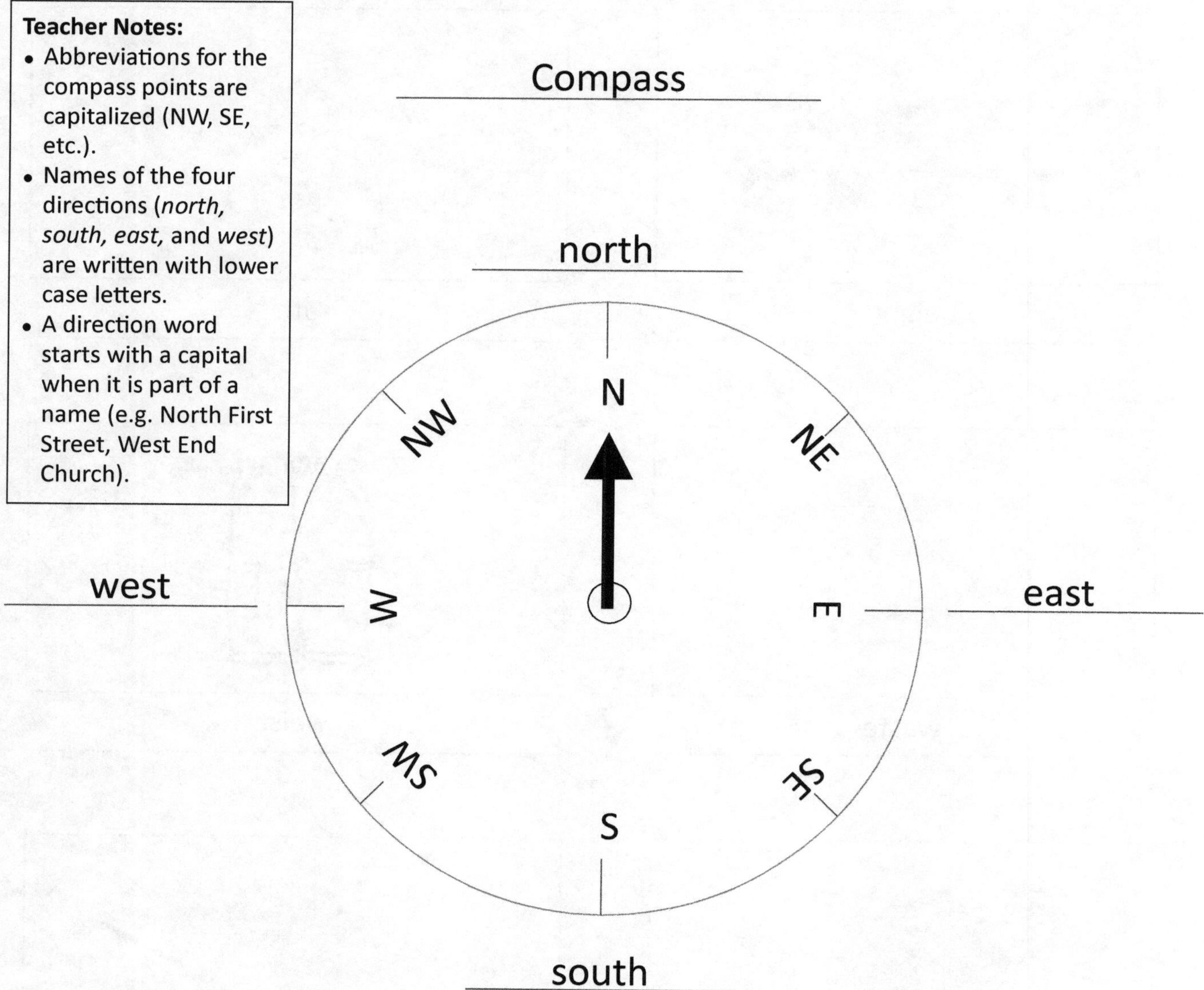

A compass with a magnetic needle pointing north can direct us where to go.

1. An ***antonym*** is a word that means the ***opposite*** of something else. For example, *aunt & uncle* or *friend & enemy* are ***antonyms***.
2. Read the words in the first column. Which of your spelling words are the ***antonyms***? Write them in the second column.
3. Are there some left that you're not sure about? Listen as your teacher reads your spelling words to you. Write the last ones.

Antonyms	Spelling Words
private	public
nearer	farther
indirect	direct
underside	surface
feel at ease	worry
insufficient	enough
north	south
after	until
arrive	depart
attic	cellar
all	none
army	navy

4. Write a sentence using one of the ***antonyms*** listed above and then rewrite the sentence using the spelling word that means the ***opposite***. You'll have two sentences with ***opposite*** meanings when you're done. Underline the ***antonyms*** in each sentence.

Answers will vary.

Examples: The most direct road will take me north.

The most indirect road will take me south.

1. Write your spelling words as your teacher dictates them.
2. When you're done with your quiz, your words will now be in ***alphabetical*** order!
3. Correct any errors.

Letters	Spelling Words	Letters	Spelling Words
c	cellar	n	navy
	confirm		none
d	depart		north
	directs	p	public
e	enough	q	quarter
f	farther		quite
	forty	s	south
	fourteen		surface
	fourth	u	until
k	knew	w	worry

TEACHER NOTES:

1. Start this activity by giving a quiz on List O-3, having your student write the words on 3x5 cards.
2. Correct any errors.
3. Demonstrate how to alphabetize the words using the cards. All words need to be alphabetized, even when they start with the same letter.
4. Collect the cards once they are in *alphabetical* order.
5. As a final quiz, dictate the words again, having him write them on this worksheet. The result will be an *alphabetized* list of all 20 spelling words.
6. Have him correct any spelling errors.

1. Take a quiz on your spelling words in the first column. Correct your work.
2. Add ***prefixes*** to your words to create ***derivatives***. Each word can have at least one ***derivative***.
3. Notice that you have several ***prefixes*** that mean ***not***. Be sure you are choosing the correct one for that spelling word. If you're not sure, look it up in the dictionary.

Prefixes							
dis-	opposite of	*im-*	not	*mid-*	middle	*pre-*	before
in-	not	*ir-*	not	*mis-*	wrong	*un-*	not

Spelling Words	Derivatives
worthy	unworthy
shed	unshed
judge	misjudge, prejudge
pleasure	displeasure
appear	disappear
locate	dislocate
contained	precontained
quiet	disquiet
ocean	midocean
perfect	imperfect
figure	disfigure, prefigure, misfigure
personal	impersonal
proper	improper
regular	irregular
afraid	unafraid
shrink	preshrink
holy	unholy
holiday	preholiday
comfort	discomfort
population	mispopulation

1. An ***analogy*** is a comparison between two things.
2. Look at the first pair of words and figure out the relationship between them. Then look at the second set of words which is unfinished. They will share the same relationship as the first two. Can you finish the set?

   Car is to road as train is to ____track____.

   In this example, the comparison (or the relationship) is where a vehicle travels.
3. Below are pairs of words. The first pair relate to one another in some way. Use that same relationship to complete the second pair.
4. Use your spelling words from this week's list to complete each set of ***analogies***.

Inhale is to exhale as enlarge is to ____shrink____.

Irritate is to encourage as annoy is to ____comfort____.

Routine is to special as regular day is to ____holiday____.

Bad is to good as sinful is to ____holy____.

Peaceful is to scared as calm is to ____afraid____.

Loud is to silent as noise is to ____quiet____.

Extra Credit: Create two analogies of your own.

________ is to ________ as

________ is to ________.

________ is to ________ as

________ is to ________.

1. Take a quiz on your spelling words in the first column.
2. Correct your work to be sure everything is spelled correctly.
3. Add the ***suffix -ing*** to your words to create ***derivatives*** — a word that has word parts added to a ***root word***. Watch for the E's Dropping Rule!

Spelling Words	Derivatives
confuse	confusing
endure	enduring
project	projecting
reject	rejecting
skirt	skirting
canoe	canoeing
elect	electing
picnic	picnicking
retire	retiring
raise	raising

Teacher Note:
All of the rules have to work together, which means that sometimes one will take precedence over another.

canoeing - retain the E as the need for clarity overrides rule #16

picnicking - change the C to CK to separate C and I —see rule #2

4. Write a sentence using one of your new ***derivatives***.

Answers will vary.

Examples: I had a lot of fun canoeing with my brother.

I find that subject quite confusing when I do not study.

1. Take a quiz on your spelling words in the first column.
2. Correct your work to be sure everything is spelled correctly.
3. Add the ***suffix -ly*** to your words to create ***adverbs***. These are words that modify ***verbs***, ***adjectives***, or other ***adverbs***.
4. Sometimes when you add the ***-ly suffix***, you create a double consonant. Watch for these.
5. The last two words look like they break the E's Dropping rule, but they don't! Can you explain why?

Spelling Words	Adverbs
distant	distantly
sweeping	sweepingly
sudden	suddenly
royal	royally
public	publicly
chief	chiefly
quiet	quietly
personal	personally
perfect	perfectly
regular	regularly
true	truly ← **Teacher Note:** See WG p. 127 and SWR p. 146
whole	wholly ←

6. Write a sentence using one of your new ***adverbs***.

Answers will vary.

Examples: He suddenly had a great idea.

I am wholly in favor of his plan.

1. Good writers play with language to make it more interesting and fun for the reader.
2. One technique you can add to your writing is called ***alliteration,*** which is where a ***sound*** is repeated at the beginning of several words of a sentence. Read this sentence and listen for the ***sound*** that is repeated.

   The cat called for her kittens when they cried for milk.
3. As your teacher reads your spelling words from Lists O-5 & O-6, listen to the first ***sound*** of each word. Does it start with one of the ***sounds*** below? If so, write it under the appropriate sound. (The letter inside the slashes indicates a ***sound***, not necessarily the letter at the beginning of the word.)

/k/	/d/	/p/	/r/
confuse	during	project	reject
canoe	distant	picnic	retire
creature	district	palace	raise
company	duty	penny	remains
curtain	don't		royal
			resurrection
			rather
			restrain
			redeem

Teacher Note: Read all the words from Wise Lists O-5 and O-6, ***in the order they occur in the WG***, having your student listen for and record the words that start with these ***sounds.***

4. Write two sentences that include ***alliteration***, using some of the words above. Each sentence needs to include <u>at least three</u> of these spelling words, but you're free to add more words to really saturate the sentence with your sound. (Did you hear that ***alliteration***?)

Answers will vary.

Example: During the distant district meeting, I didn't go home.

His project will take place at the royal palace during the picnic.

1. As your teacher dictates your spelling words, decide if the word is a ***noun.***
2. If the word is a ***noun***, write it in its ***plural*** form in the part of the ***Plurals Rule*** it is following.
3. If the word is not a ***noun***, write it in the chart at the bottom of the page.
4. Correct your work to be sure everything is spelled correctly.

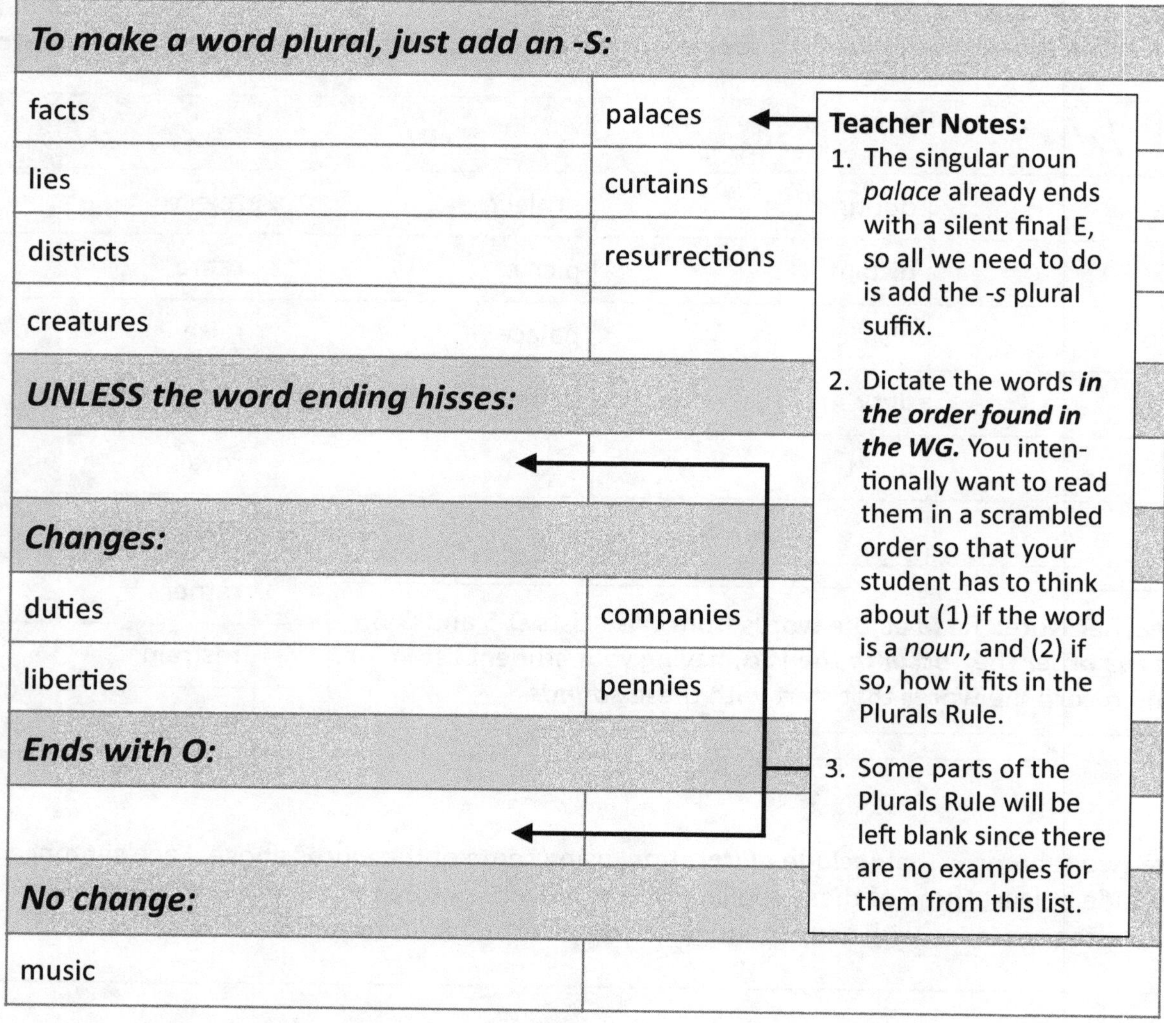

To make a word plural, just add an -S:	
facts	palaces
lies	curtains
districts	resurrections
creatures	
UNLESS the word ending hisses:	
Changes:	
duties	companies
liberties	pennies
Ends with O:	
No change:	
music	

Teacher Notes:

1. The singular noun *palace* already ends with a silent final E, so all we need to do is add the -*s* plural suffix.
2. Dictate the words ***in the order found in the WG.*** You intentionally want to read them in a scrambled order so that your student has to think about (1) if the word is a *noun,* and (2) if so, how it fits in the Plurals Rule.
3. Some parts of the Plurals Rule will be left blank since there are no examples for them from this list.

Not Nouns	
lying	don't
rather	stir
restrain	everything
instead	redeem

Wise Guide Enrichment Activity Worksheets

Lists P-1 to P-7

1. Take a quiz on some of your spelling words in the first column.
2. Correct your work.
3. Find which ***suffixes*** below can be added to your words to form ***derivatives***. Will you create a double consonant by adding a ***suffix***?

Suffixes	
-less	without
-ly	in a manner, like
-ment	act, or state, or condition of being
-ness	quality, state, or condition of being

Spelling Words	Derivatives
important	importantly
button	buttonless
human	humanly, humanness
match	matchless
settle	settlement
regard	regardless
value	valueless
usual	usually, usualness
fortune	fortuneless
count	countless

Teacher Note:
If the student is new to this kind of activity, use the *suffix* cards from WG p. 98 with flash cards with the spelling words to demonstrate how to mix and match to form real English *derivatives*.

4. Write a sentence using one of your new ***derivatives***.

Answers will vary.

Examples: I enjoyed that book, but more importantly, it helped change my life.

Regardless of the task, I will always try to do my best.

List P-1 Prefixes

ANSWER KEY

1. Take a quiz on some of your new spelling words. Correct your work.
2. Add following ***prefixes*** to your words to create ***derivatives***. All but four of the words can have more than one ***prefix***.
3. Use your dictionary to make sure you're using the correct ***prefix*** for that word.

Prefixes	
mid-	middle
pre-	before
re-	again, once more
super-	above, over

Spelling Words	Derivatives	Derivatives
button	rebutton	prebutton, prebuttoned
human	superhuman	
match	rematch	midmatch
settle	resettle	presettle
value	revalue, supervalue,	prevalue
count	recount	midcount
caught	recaught	
taught	retaught	pretaught
flight	preflight	midflight
trial	pretrial, midtrial,	retrial
scale	rescale	
double	redouble	

Teacher Notes:

1. To use *pre-* with the base word *button,* we might add the *suffix -ed.*
2. If the student is new to this kind of activity, use the *prefix* cards from WG p. 116 with flash cards with the spelling words to demonstrate how to mix and match to form real English *derivatives*.

1. Listed below are ***prefixes*** that can be added to words to create ***antonyms,*** or words that mean the ***opposite*** of the spelling word.
2. You'll notice that all the ***prefixes*** have similar meanings, but each spelling word can only use a certain ***prefix*** to create a ***negative antonym***. Some words can use more than one of these ***prefixes***, depending on the meaning of the new word.
3. Look at your List P-1 words in your Learning Log. Add the ***prefixes*** to your spelling words to create ***negative antonyms.*** Write the ***derivative*** under the ***prefix*** you used.
4. Use your dictionary to check your answers.

Negative Prefixes			
de-	to do the opposite	*mis-*	wrong
dis-	opposite of	*non-*	not, opposite of, lack of
in-	not	*un-*	not

de-	**in-**	**non-**	**un-**
devalue	inhuman	nonhuman	unimportant
		nonsupport	unbutton
dis-	**mis-**		unmatched
disregard	mismatch		unsettled
discount	misfortune		unusual
disrepair	mistaught		uncounted
disfavor	mistrial		unrepaired
			uncaught
			untaught
			unscaled
			unknown
			undoubled

1. Take a quiz on some of your new spelling words in the first column.
2. Correct your quiz so that everything is spelled correctly.
3. Combine your spelling words with the ***suffixes*** to create two ***derivatives*** for each spelling word. What rule will you use to add endings?

Suffixes				
-able	*-(a)tion*	*-ed*	*-ible*	*-ing*

Spelling Words	Derivatives	Derivatives
notice	noticed, noticing,	noticeable
obtain	obtained, obtaining,	obtainable
escape	escaped, escaping,	escapable
visit	visited, visiting,	visitation
coast	coasted,	coasting
complicate	complicated, complicating,	complication
desire	desired, desiring,	desirable
produce	produced, producing,	producible, production
trace	traced, tracing,	traceable
cough	coughed	coughing
style	styled, styling,	stylable
retreat	retreated	retreating
pattern	patterned, patterning,	patternable
shield	shielded,	shielding
oblige	obliged, obliging,	obligation
trouble	troubled	troubling
laugh	laughed, laughing,	laughable

Teacher Note: While multiple possibilities are listed, the student only needs to write two derivatives for each spelling word.

1. Take a quiz on some of your spelling words in the first column.
2. Correct your work to be sure everything is spelled correctly.
3. Add the ***suffix -ing*** to each of your words in the second column to create a ***derivative***. Which words need the 1-1-1 or 2-1-1 rules before you can add this ending?
4. In the last column write the rule you used (1-1-1 or 2-1-1). If you can't use either of them, write the letter (***a, b, c,*** or ***d***) that explains why you will ***not*** use one of these rules.

a. not a single vowel
b. not a single consonant
c. no consonant sound
d. accent on the first syllable

Spelling Words	Derivatives	Rule? Why Not?
wait	waiting	a
quit	quitting	1-1-1
thumb	thumbing	b
blur	blurring	1-1-1
lack	lacking	b
signal	signaling	d
level	leveling	d
admit	admitting	2-1-1
shadow	shadowing	c
travel	traveling	d
acquit	acquitting	2-1-1

Teacher Notes:
1. Dictate the bonus word ***acquit*** OR the review word ***visit*** (*visiting* - d).
2. See WG p. 137 for more on British versions of some of these *derivatives*.

1. As your teacher dictates your spelling words, write them next to the letter that starts that word.
2. Some of your spelling words start with the same letter. As you hear these, write them on the lower part of the page under the appropriate letter. Once you have all of the words that start with that letter, add them to the upper chart in ***alphabetical*** order.
3. When you're done with your quiz, all your words will now be in ***alphabetical*** order.
4. Correct any errors.

Letters	Spelling Words	Letters	Spelling Words
a	admit	p	prison
b	blur	q	quit
c	coward	r	rapid
e	election		reddish
g	grief	s	shadow
l	lack		signal
	language	t	thumb
	level		travel
m	Mrs.	v	verb
n	noun	w	wait

Teacher Notes:

1. Read the List P-3 words ***as they are listed in the WG.*** Your student needs to select where to write each word and which words need to be written on the lower part of the page first to determine correct alphabetical order.
2. The words below are in the order they will be written as you dictate the words. Let him determine that these words should be written here before he adds them to the alphabetical chart in the correct order.

l
lack
level
language

r
rapid
reddish

s
signal
shadow

t
thumb
travel

1. As your teacher dictates your spelling words, write them next to the letter that starts that word.
2. Some of your spelling words start with the same letter. As you hear these, write them on the lower part of the page under the appropriate letter. Once you have all of the words that start with that letter, add them to the upper chart in ***alphabetical*** order.
3. When you're done with your quiz, all your words will now be in ***alphabetical*** order.
4. Correct any errors.

Letters	Spelling Words	Letters	Spelling Words
a	amount	n	newspaper
	animal		ninth
c	caterpillar	o	o'clock
	complaint	s	sail
	curious		sale
d	decimal		several
e	equal		since
h	hearse		strength
	hundred		subtract
n	nearly	w	which

Teacher Notes:

1. Read the List P-4 words ***as they are listed in the WG.*** Your student will select where to write each word and which words need to be written on the lower part of the page first to determine correct *alphabetical* order.
2. The words below are in the order they will be written as you dictate the words. Let him determine that these words should be written here before he adds them to the *alphabetical* chart in the correct order.

a
animal
amount

h
hundred
hearse

s
sale
subtract
several
since
sail
strength

c
curious
complaint
caterpillar

n
nearly
ninth
newspaper

1. Take a quiz on some review words and some of your new spelling words.
2. Correct your quiz so that everything is spelled correctly.
3. Combine your spelling words with the review words to create one ***compound word*** for each spelling word.

Review Words				
bed	dish	hold	oil	pot
broad	head	man	over	way

Spelling Words	Compound Words
strong	headstrong, stronghold
entrance	entranceway
cloth	broadcloth, dishcloth, oilcloth
spend	overspend
cattle	cattleman
steel	steelhead
view	overview
pie	potpie
spread	bedspread, overspread

Teacher Note: Although multiple options are listed for some words, only one *compound word* is necessary for each spelling word.

4. Write a sentences using one of your ***compound words*** and your new spelling words.

Answers will vary.

Example: The cattleman came through the entranceway on a horse.

We can get an overview of the problem by looking at it a day later.

1. Take a quiz on some of this week's spelling words in the first column. Correct your quiz.
2. We add the ***suffixes -er*** and ***-est*** to ***adjectives*** to express ***comparison***.

Mary is **tall.** Sue is **taller** than Mary. Tom is the **tallest** of all.

-er more of — *comparing two*

-est the most — *comparing three or more*

3. As you add the suffix endings your spelling words, watch out for the Y's Exchanging rule.

Positive Degree Adjectives	**Comparative Degree** Comparing with *-er*	**Superlative Degree** the "most" with *-est*
lengthy	lengthier	lengthiest
loud	louder	loudest
naughty	naughtier	naughtiest
hungry	hungrier	hungriest
heavy	heavier	heaviest
brief	briefer	briefest
simple	simpler	simplest
guilty	guiltier	guiltiest
slow	slower	slowest
strong	stronger	strongest

4. Write a sentences using one of your ***comparative adjectives*** and another one using a ***superlative adjective***. Try to include new or recent spelling words.

Answers will vary.

Example: His speech was lengthier than usual.

His dog was the hungriest of the pack.

1. Take a quiz on some of this week's spelling words in the first column. Correct your quiz.
2. Each of the words you wrote could be used as an ***adjective***, a word that describes a ***noun***.
3. The ***suffix -ness*** means *the quality of* or *the act of.* When added to a word, it changes that word into a noun. Add the ***suffix -ness*** to each of the spelling words.
4. Two of your derivatives have an internal change to take on this meaning instead of adding the ***suffix -ness***. Do you know these new words?
5. Watch out for the Y's Exchanging rule.

Spelling Word Adjectives	**Add *-ness*** or word with similar meaning
lengthy	lengthiness
loud	loudness
naughty	naughtiness
hungry	hungriness
heavy	heaviness
brief	**brevity**
simple	simpleness
guilty	guiltiness
slow	slowness
strong	**strength**

Teacher Note:
brevity = the quality of being brief
strength = the quality of being strong
These two words do not use the *-ness* suffix.

6. Write a sentences using one of your ***-ness nouns*** and your new spelling words.

Answers will vary.

Example: The heaviness of his lids finally overtook him, and he simply fell asleep.

His guiltiness could be viewed by everyone in the room.

1. Good writers use ***vivid words***. These are words that are more expressive or more precise. They help the reader understand more clearly what the author is trying to communicate.
2. Take a quiz on your new spelling words below. Write the words that refer to ***people*** in the first column.
3. In the second column write the words that refer to how someone ***speaks*** to someone else. You will need to make sure your ***verbs*** match their ***subjects*** by adding the appropriate ***suffix*** (***-s or -es***). Do you need to use any spelling rules to add these endings?
4. Correct your quiz to be sure everything is spelled correctly.

Person	Speaks
cousin	exhorts
passenger	counsels
nurse	answers
mayor	imitates
tailor	corrects
daughter	commits
guest	approves
nephew	shares
husband	replies
clerk	whispers

Teacher Note: Determine how many sentences you want your student to write and fill in the blank.

5. On a separate piece of paper, write _________ sentences by combining one of your words for a ***person*** with one of your words for ***speaks***. Add adjectives to be even more descriptive. Be sure to start with a capital letter and end with the appropriate punctuation (. ? !).

1. An ***analogy*** is a comparison between two things.
2. Look at the first pair of words and figure out the relationship between them. Then look at the second set of words which is unfinished. They will share the same relationship as the first two. Can you finish the set?

Red is to strawberry as yellow is to banana or lemon.

In this example, the comparison (or the relationship) is the color of a fruit.

3. Below are pairs of words. The first pair relate to one another in some way. Use that same relationship to complete the second pair.
4. Use your spelling words from this week's list to complete each set of ***analogies***.

Country is to president as city is to mayor.

God is to man as create is to imitate.

Loudest is to softest as shout is to whisper.

Woman is to man as wife is to husband.

Dentist is to hygienist as doctor is to nurse.

Mother is to son as father is to daughter.

Ball is to athlete as needle & thread are to tailor.

Extra Credit: Create an analogy of your own.

____________ is to ____________ as

____________ is to ____________.

1. Take a quiz on some of your spelling words in the first column. Correct your work.
2. Each of these words can be used as a ***present tense verb***.
3. Write the ***past tense*** version of each of your words in the second column. Which words need the E's Dropping, Y's Exchanging, or 2-1-1 rules before you can add the ED ending?
4. In the last column write the code for the rule you used if any.

a. word + ending
b. E's Dropping
c. Y's Exchanging
d. 2-1-1

Present Tense Verbs	Past Tense Verbs	Rule?
exhort	exhorted	a
counsel	counseled	a
answer	answered	a
imitate	imitated	b
correct	corrected	a
commit	committed	d
approve	approved	b
share	shared	b
reply	replied	c
whisper	whispered	a

5. Write a sentences using one of your ***past tense verbs*** and your new spelling words.

Answers will vary.

Example: He committed himself to our group's election project.

She whispered her reply into Mother's ears.

1. An ***antonym*** is a word that means the ***opposite*** of something else. For example, *add & subtract* or *strength & weakness* are antonyms.
2. Read the words in the first column. Which of your spelling words are the ***antonyms***? Write them in the second column.
3. Are there some left that you're not sure about? Listen as your teacher reads your spelling words to you. Write the last ones.

Antonyms	Spelling Words
son	daughter
driver	passenger
ask	answer
hostess	guest
citizen	mayor
conductor	passenger
wife	husband
niece	nephew
reject	approve
wrong	correct
shout	whisper
originate	imitate

4. Write a sentence using one of the ***antonyms*** listed above and then rewrite the sentence using the spelling word that means the ***opposite***. You'll have two sentences with ***opposite*** meanings when you're done. Underline the ***antonyms*** in each sentence.

Answers will vary.

Examples: My <u>niece</u> liked the gift I gave <u>her</u> for <u>her</u> birthday.

My <u>nephew</u> liked the gift I gave <u>him</u> for <u>his</u> birthday.

1. The first part of the ***Plurals Rule*** is written below.
2. Listen as your teacher reads your spelling words to you.
3. If the word could be used as a ***noun***, write the ***plural*** form of it, placing the word under the appropriate part of the ***Plurals Rule***.
4. If the word could not be used as a ***noun***, write it in the appropriate section at the bottom of the page, depending on what part of speech it is.

To make a word plural, just add an -S:	
wrongs	vacations
engines	degrees
cabbages	voyages
awes	empires
UNLESS the word ending hisses:	
losses	
Changes:	
families	cities
beauties	industries

Adjectives	Adverbs
beautiful	though
awful	
careful	

Verbs	Prepositions
enjoy	beneath
carries	

1. As your teacher dictates your spelling words, write them next to the letter that starts that word.
2. Some of your spelling words start with the same letter. As you hear these, write them on the lower part of the page under the appropriate letter. Once you have all of the words that start with that letter, add them to the upper chart in ***alphabetical*** order.
3. When you're done with your quiz, all your words will now be in ***alphabetical*** order.
4. Correct any errors.

Letters	Spelling Words	Letters	Spelling Words
a	awe	e	empire
	awful		engine
b	beautiful		enjoy
	beauty	f	family
	beneath	i	industry
c	cabbage	l	loss
	careful	t	though
	carries	v	vacation
	cities		voyage
d	degree	w	wrong

Teacher Notes:

1. Read the List P-7 words ***as they are listed in the WG.*** Your student will select where to write each word and which words need to be written on the lower part of the page first to determine correct *alphabetical* order.
2. The words below are in the order they will be written as you dictate the words. Let him determine that these words should be written here before he adds them to the *alphabetical* chart in the correct order.

a
awe
awful

b
beauty
beneath
beautiful

c
careful
cabbage
carries
cities

e
engine
enjoy
empire

v
vacation
voyage

Hill and ***kill*** look and sound alike, but are not related in meaning.

Words in the ***hill*** family include ***hillside, hilly,*** and ***hilltop*** because they relate back to the base word ***hill***.

1. Below you will find some of your spelling words or their ***root words***. Fill in the missing information (***root words*** and/or ***derivatives***) for each word. Each ***root word*** can have at least two ***derivatives***.
2. Watch for spelling rules that help you as you add endings.

Prefix
over-

Suffixes							
-al	*-(e)s*	*-er*	*-ing*	*-ly*	*-ness*	*-ship*	*-y*
-ed	*-eer*	*-ful*	*-less*	*-ment*	*-or*	*-some*	*-zen*

Teacher Note:
Words in **bold** below have been included on the student's version of this page.

Root Words	Derivatives	Derivatives
family	familial	families
care	**careful,** carefulness,	overcareful, carefully, careless
beauty	**beautiful**	beautify, beautifully
wrong	wrongly, wronged, wrongfully,	wronging
engine	engineer, engineering,	engineered
awe	awesome, overawed, awful,	awfully
joy	joyful(ness), joyfully, overjoy(ed),	enjoy(ed), enjoyment
voyage	voyager	voyages
carry	**carries**	carrier, carried
city	**cities**	citizen(ship), citify, citified
empire	empires	emperor
industry	industrial, industriousness,	industries

Wise Guide
Enrichment Activity
Worksheets

Lists Q-1 to Q-6

1. Take a quiz on this week's words in the first column. Correct your work.
2. Add the ***prefixes*** below to your words to form ***derivatives***. The meanings of these ***prefixes*** are listed for you on page B36 in your Learning Log.
3. All but two of your words can have at least two ***derivatives.*** Use a dictionary to check your answers.

Prefixes												
dis-	*in-*	*inter-*	*im-*	*mid-*	*mis-*	*non-*	*pre-*	*pro-*	*re-*	*sub-*	*trans-*	*un-*

Spelling Word	Derivative	Derivative
claim	midclaim, reclaim, proclaim,	disclaimer
measure	premeasure	remeasure
represent	misrepresent, nonrepresentable,	prerepresent, unrepresentable
position	disposition, reposition,	imposition
suppose	presuppose, missupposing,	unsupposable
arrange	rearrange, disarrange,	prearrange
similar	dissimilar, nonsimilar,	non similarly
continue	discontinue	noncontinuable
appoint	reappoint, disappoint,	preappointed
touch	retouch	intertouch
action	inaction, interaction, reaction,	transaction
importance	preimportance	unimportance
justice	injustice	
section	midsection	unsectioned
connect	disconnect, interconnect,	misconnect, reconnect, subconnect
connection	disconnection, misconnection,	preconnection, reconnection
field	infield, midfield	unfielded
direction	misdirection	predirection
term	interterm	midterm
veil	unveil	

Teacher Note: Although multiple options are listed for some words, only two *derivatives* are necessary for each spelling word.

Combine your ***prefixes*** and ***suffixes*** with the base word ***act*** to form as many ***derivatives*** as you can.

act *derivatives*		

Teacher Notes:

1. Use the *suffix* and *prefix* cards from WG pp. 98 and 116 with a 3x5 card for *act.*
2. See the *Alpha List* p. 72 and SWR pp. 130-131 for more on *derivatives* that can be formed from the base word *act.* There are 85 possibilities while this page allows for 36 answers.

1. Take a quiz on six of your spelling words in the first column of the first chart and four more of your words at the bottom of the page in the second chart. One word is in both places.
2. Correct your quiz so that everything is spelled correctly.
3. At the top of the first column, write the ***part of speech*** for the words you wrote. If you're not sure, see B27 in your Learning Log for the ***eight parts of speech***.
4. Add the ***suffixes -tion*** or ***-ment*** to each of these words in the second column to make an English ***derivative*** for each word.
5. What new ***part of speech*** did you create? Write that at the top of that column.

Verbs	Nouns
represent	representation
arrange	arrangement
continue	continuation
appoint	appointment
connect	connection
direct	direction

6. Some words can be used as different ***parts of speech***, depending on what they mean or how they are being used.
7. On a separate page, write a sentence for each of the following words. The word will be used twice in each sentence, once as a ***noun*** and then again as a ***verb***.
8. Underline your spelling words in each sentence.

claim	field
veil	direct

1. As your teacher dictates your spelling words, write them in their ***plural*** form in the part of the ***Plurals Rule*** they are following.
2. Correct your work to be sure everything is spelled correctly.

Teacher Note:
Dictate the spelling words ***in the following order***.

prompt
private
branch
primary
factory
murder
gentleman
self
calf
command
beggar
property

To make a word plural, just add an -S:	
prompts	beggars
murders	privates
commands	
UNLESS the word ending hisses:	
branches	
Changes: ***f → v***	***y → i***
selves	primaries
calves	factories
	properties
Internal change:	
gentlemen	

3. Write a sentence using one of your new ***plurals***.

Answers will vary.

Examples: Several factories opened up in our town.

The branches on the tree fell off during the storm.

1. Take a quiz on your spelling words below. Correct your work.
2. An ***adjective*** describes or modifies a ***noun***, which is a person, place, thing, or idea.
3. Write the ***part of speech*** at the top of each column.

Adjectives	Nouns
whose	branch
quick	primary
entire	factory
terrible	murder
prompt	gentleman
wonderful	self
select	calf
calm	command
smooth	beggar
private	property

Teacher Notes:

1. Dictate the spelling words ***in the order found in the WG*** so that you fill the first column and then the second column.
2. If you have not worked with your student on the eight parts of speech, now is a good time to fill in Learning Log p. B27, or at least the definitions for *adjectives* and *nouns* and add some samples from this worksheet onto p. B28.
3. Continue this assignment using *adjective-noun* combinations from List Q-2 on the Adjectives Sentences worksheet on p. 95.

1. Look over your ***adjective-noun*** combinations that you wrote on the Adjectives worksheet.
2. Write ________ sentences, using these ***adjective-noun*** combinations.
3. Underline your ***adjective-noun*** combinations.

Teacher Notes:

1. Determine how many sentences you would like your student to write and fill that number in the blank for #2.
2. If your student tends to write simple or short sentences, consider having him to add a *prepositional phrase* (see worksheet p. 23) or an *opening adverbial clause* (see worksheet p. 109) to each sentence.

1. Take a quiz on some of your new spelling words in the first column. Correct your work.
2. Write your spelling words again in the second column as an ***adverb*** with the ***-ly suffix***.
3. Do you need to use one of your spelling rules before adding the ***suffix***? Or can you just add it to the end of the word?

Spelling Words	Adverbs
quick	quickly
entire	entirely
terrible	terribly*
prompt	promptly
wonderful	wonderfully**
select	selectly
calm	calmly
smooth	smoothly
private	privately
primary	primarily
gentleman	gentlemanly
beggar	beggarly

Teacher Notes:

*Even though you're adding a *consonant suffix* to *terrible*, you will merely drop the E to add *-y*. This helps avoid the more cumbersome *ter-ri-ble-ly.* The tendency is to find the easiest way to say words.

**When you add the *-ly suffix* to a word already ending with the letter L, you create a double consonant in the derivative. Does your student recognize this pattern?

4. Write a sentence using one of your new ***adverbs***.

Answers will vary.

Examples: The boat sailed smoothly through the sea.

He was terribly upset when the heavy branch fell on his car.

1. A ***synonym*** is a word that has a ***similar meaning*** as another word. For example, *quick* & *fast* and *connect* & *fasten* can be ***synonyms***.
2. When words ***rhyme***, they end with the ***same sounds***. For example, *field* and *yield* ***rhyme***.
3. Below are some word puzzles that include ***rhyming synonyms***. Use the words in the Word Bank to finish the first set of word puzzles. The first one is done for you.

An ill bird is a **sick** __chick__.

A joyful papa is a **glad** __dad__.

A sulky boy is a **mad** __lad__.

A midday beverage is a **lunch** __punch__.

A quick explosion is a **fast** __blast__.

A large hog is a **big** __pig__.

A rodent home is a **mouse** __house__.

Word Bank	
dad	pig
blast	lad
house	punch

4. Here are some more word puzzles that need words from List Q-2 to complete them. The ***rhyming synonym*** is in bold.

A **damp tramp** is a wet __beggar__.

A **sweet treat** is a __wonderful__ dessert.

A **hill kill** is a mountain __murder__.

A **main stain** is a __primary__ blotch.

A **scream dream** is a __terrible__ nightmare.

A divided cow is a **half** __calf__.

A steady hand is a __calm__ **palm**.

A slippery glide is a __smooth__ **move**.

A rapid kiss is a __quick__ **lick**.

Unidentified footwear are __whose__ **shoes**?

1. Take a quiz on some review words and some of your new spelling words.
2. Correct your quiz so that everything is spelled correctly.
3. Combine your spelling words with the review words to create one ***compound word*** for each spelling word.

Review Words				
bone	ever	hand	less	taking
drop	foot	hearted	over	under

Spelling Words	Compound Words
running	overrunning
crowd	overcrowd
dew	dewdrop
written	handwritten, underwritten
whom	whomever
statement	overstatement, understatement
exercise	overexercise
breath	breathless, breathtaking
tender	tenderfoot, tenderhearted
ankle	anklebone
confidence	overconfidence
weapon	weaponless

Teacher Note: Although multiple options are listed for some words, only one *compound word* is necessary for each spelling word.

4. Write a sentence using one of your new ***compound words***.

Answers will vary.

Examples: Will your note to Grandmother be handwritten?

His overconfidence was his downfall.

1. Take a quiz on some of this week's words in the first column. Correct your work.
2. Add the ***suffixes*** below to your words to form ***derivatives***. All of these words except one can make at least two ***derivatives*** each.
3. Can you just add the endings, or do you need to use a spelling rule first?

Suffixes		
-ance	*-en*	*-ing*
-ed	*-est*	*-ly*
-er	*-ful*	*-y*

Spelling Words	Derivatives	Derivatives
ledge	ledged, ledger,	ledging **E's Dropping**
toss	tossed	tossing
tender	tendered, tendering,	tenderly
run ←	runner	running **1-1-1**
allow	allowance, allowed,	allowing
crowd	crowded	crowding
firm	firmed, firmer, firmest,	firming, firmly
dew	dewed, dewing,	dewy
writ ←	written	**1-1-1**
pride	prided, prideful	priding **E's Dropping**

Teacher Notes:

1. Dictate the base words ***run*** and ***writ*** for the new spelling words (*running* and *written*) in order to demonstrate why these derivatives are spelled the way they are.
2. If you want to introduce this assignment, per the instructions at the top of WG p. 153, you could walk the student through the process of adding the *ED ending* to each word. Use *runner* and *written* for those two derivatives since they won't take the *ED ending*.
3. The verb *pride* cannot take the *suffixes -er, -est,* or *-ly* as these would be added to the related word *proud.*
4. The rules used to form the derivatives are noted above for the teacher in **bold**. The student does not need to note these, only to use the rules appropriately.

Use your new spelling words and a New King James Version Bible to complete the List Q-3 Cross-Word Puzzle.

> **Teacher Note:** If you don't have a New King James Version of the Bible, your student can use www.biblegateway.com to look up the verses. Only this translations gives the correct answers.

Across

1. Then the man said, "The woman __whom__ You gave to be with me... (Gen. 3:12)
3. And he took him by the right hand and lifted him up, and immediately his feet and __ankle__ bones received strength. (Acts 3:7)
5. For He shall grow up before Him as a __tender__ plant. (Is. 53:2)
6. And when the layer of __dew__ lifted, there, on the surface of the wilderness, was a small round substance, as fine as frost on the ground. (Ex. 16:14)
9. Also Isaac's servants dug in the valley, and found a well of __running__ water there. (Gen. 26:19)
14. 'You shall take some of its blood and put it on the four horns of the altar, on the four corners of the __ledge__, and on the rim around it; thus you shall cleanse it and make atonement for it. (Ez. 43:20)
15. But reject profane and old wives' fables, and __exercise__ yourself toward godliness. (1 Tim. 4:7)
16. And though its waves __toss__ to and fro, Yet they cannot prevail... (Jer. 5:22)
17. When __pride__ comes, then comes shame; but with the humble is wisdom. (Prov. 11:2)

Down

1. Those who built on the wall, and those who carried burdens, loaded themselves so that with one hand they worked at construction, and with the other held a __weapon__. (Neh. 4:17)
2. Let your light so shine before men, that they may see your good words and __glorify__ your Father in heaven. (Matt. 5:16)
4. But they did not understand the __statement__ which He spoke to them. (Luke 2:50)
7. It is better to trust in the Lord than to put __confidence__ in man. (Psalm 118:8)
8. This will be __written__ for the generation to come, that a people yet to be created may praise the Lord. (Psalm 102:18)
10. And the Lord God formed man of the dust of the ground, and breathed into his nostrils the __breath__ of life; and man became a living being. (Gen. 2:7)
11. But Sihon would not __allow__ Israel to pass through his territory. (Num. 21:23)
12. When she heard about Jesus, she came behind Him in the __crowd__ and touched His garment. (Mark 5:27)
13. Take __firm__ hold of instruction, do not let go; Keep her, for she is your life. (Prov. 4:13)

Use the clues on p. 100 along with a New King James Version Bible to complete this puzzle that contains your new spelling words.

1 whom / weapon
2 glorify
3 ankle
4 statement
5 tender
6 dew
7 confidence
8 written
9 running
10 breath
11 allow
12 crowd
13 firm
14 ledge
15 exercise
16 toss
17 pride

1. A ***pronoun*** is a word that replaces a ***noun***. A ***subject pronoun*** tells us the person or thing that is doing the action and the ***object pronoun*** tells us the person or thing that is receiving the action.
2. Use the sample sentences to fill in the ***Pronoun*** chart below for ***singular pronouns*** (only one).
3. ***Relative pronouns*** also act like ***nouns*** and can fill the role of ***subject*** or ***object pronouns***. Add these to the chart as well.

_______ *will hop.* *Jill gave the toy to _______.*

Person		Subject	Object
1st		I	me
2nd		you	you
3rd	M	he	him
	F	she	her
	N	it	it
Relative		who	whom

4. Write two sentences your teacher dictates below. Rewrite each sentence as a question and change the regular ***subject*** or ***object pronoun*** in each sentence into the appropriate ***relative pronoun***. Finally, write your own sentence using one of these ***relative pronouns***.

1. **<u>She</u> will go to the party with the gentleman.**
2. Who will go to the party with the gentleman?
3. **The girl tossed the ball to <u>him</u>.**
4. The girl tossed the ball to whom?
5. Answers will vary.

Teacher Notes:

1. Dictate sentences #1 & #3 shown in **bold** to the left.
2. To help your student use the correct *relative pronoun,* have him identify the *pronoun* in the sentence you dictated (underlined for the teacher here).
3. Ask if it's being used as a *subject* or *object pronoun.*
4. Replace it with the appropriate *relative pronoun* (*who* or *whom*) in sentences #2 & #4.
5. *Object Pronouns* follow a *preposition* and complete the *prepositional phrase.*
   to her - to whom
   with him - with whom
   for them - for whom

1. The words ***a*** and ***an*** are ***articles*** and are used before a ***noun*** or before an ***adjective*** that is describing a ***noun***.

   a touch   *a* section   *an* extra term   *an* action

2. The word ***a*** is used before a word that starts with a ***consonant sound*** whereas the word ***an*** is used before a word that starts with a ***vowel sound***.
3. Your teacher will dictate some phrases that include review and new spelling words.
4. Write these phrases on the lines below, but first add the appropriate ***article*** at the beginning of each phrase. Listen for the first ***sound*** in the first word and write ***a*** or ***an***, depending on which ***sound*** you hear.

a northern direction	**an** ankle bone
a lace veil	**a** crowded ledge
an odd position	**an** exercise room
a red measuring stick	**a** proud statement
a long field	**a** new arrest
an entire factory	**an** enclosed bill
a sleepy beggar	**a** critical attempt
an old gentleman	**a** country circus

Teacher Notes:

1. Dictate each phrase ***without*** the ***article a*** or ***an***, which are shown in **bold** above. For example, dictate *northern direction, lace veil, odd position,* etc. The student will write the entire phrase, including the *article*.
2. The review words are taken from Lists Q-1 through Q-4.

1. Take a quiz on your new spelling words and on one review word.
2. Be sure the ***verb*** matches the ***noun*** in the first column in ***number***.
3. Correct your quiz to be sure everything is spelled correctly.

Nouns	Verbs
president	presides
relative	arrests
boundary	encloses
thirteen	remember
mice	attempt
circus	awaits
critic	convicts
culture	consents
problem	relates
crowd	declares

Teacher Note:
Number words *are* typically *adjectives.* Numbers can be used as *nouns* when they are replacing the noun they would be modifying and the noun is understood. For example:
All thirteen cats slept.
OR *All thirteen slept.*

Teacher Note:
Determine how many sentences you want your student to write and fill in the blank.

Teacher Notes:
1. Dictate the *nouns* column first.
2. Next, dictate the *verbs* column as follows:

preside	*await*
arrest	*convict*
enclose	*consent*
remember	*relate*
attempt	*declare*

3. The student is to decide if the *verb* needs to be changed to match its *noun*.

4. On a separate piece of paper, write _________ sentences following these instructions:
   a. Combine one of these ***nouns*** with one of the ***verbs***. You can use the words on the same lines above or make new combinations, as long as you don't repeat any of these words.
   b. Add an appropriate ***article*** (a, an, the) before the ***noun*** in your sentences.
   c. Keep your ***verbs*** in the ***present tense*** and make sure they match their ***nouns***.
   d. Put a check mark (✓) over the article.
   e. Underline the noun from your list above once.
   f. Double underline the verb from above.
5. Here's an example.

✓
The man's relative consents to join us at dinner.

1. Good writers play with language to make it more interesting and fun for the reader.
2. One technique you can add to your writing is called ***alliteration,*** which is where a ***sound*** is repeated at the beginning of several words of a sentence. Read this sentence and listen for the ***sound*** that is repeated.

   The cat called for her kittens when they cried for milk.
3. As your teacher reads your spelling words from List Q-4, listen to the first ***sound*** of each word. Does it start with one of the ***sounds*** below? If so, write it under the appropriate sound. (The letter inside the slashes indicates a ***sound***, not necessarily the letter at the beginning of the word.)

/a/	/k/	/p/	/r/
attempt	critic	president	relative
arrest	culture	problem	relate
await	convict	preside	remember
	consent		

Teacher Note: Read all the words from Wise List Q-4, ***in the order they occur in the WG***, having your student listen for and record the words that start with these ***sounds.***

4. Using these spelling words, combine your spelling words into ***alliterative pairs*** below. The first one is done for you.
5. You can use your words multiple times to create different combinations. Make sure any ***verbs*** you use match their ***nouns*** in ***number*** and ***tense***.

attempted arrest

await arrest

arresting attempt

cultures consent

culture critic

critic convicts

president presides

president's problem

president's progress

relative relates

relative remembers

remember relatives

Teacher Note:
These are possible combinations, but your student may think of others.

1. An ***antonym*** is a word that means the ***opposite*** of something else. For example, *problem & solution* or *release & enclose* are ***antonyms***.
2. Read the words in the first column. Which of your spelling words are the ***antonyms***? Write them in the second column.
3. Are there some left that you're not sure about? Listen as your teacher reads your spelling words to you. Write the last ones.

Antonyms	Spelling Words
absent	present
subtraction	addition
diminish	magnify
release	imprison
disengage	engage
choke	breathe

4. Write a sentence using one of the ***antonyms*** listed above and then rewrite the sentence using the spelling word that means the ***opposite***. You'll have two sentences with ***opposite*** meanings when you're done. Underline the ***antonyms*** in each sentence.

Answers will vary.

Examples: Was the student absent from class?

Was the student present in class?

1. Take a quiz on some of your new spelling words in the first column. Correct your work.
2. Add the suffixes ***-ed*** and ***-ing*** to your words to create ***derivatives***. Watch out for E's Dropping and Y's Exchanging words.

Spelling Words	*-ed*	*-ing*
publish	published	publishing
manufacture	manufactured	manufacturing
imprison	imprisoned	imprisoning
present	presented	presenting
breathe	breathed	breathing
employ	employed	employing
serve	served	serving
brace	braced	bracing
magnify	magnified	magnifying
engage	engaged	engaging

3. Write two sentences using one of your new ***derivatives*** in each one.

Answers will vary.

Examples: He employed several students for the summer at his factory.

The book was quite engaging.

1. Take a quiz on your new spelling words in the first column. Correct your work.
2. Add ***suffixes*** to your words to create ***derivatives***. Watch out for E's Dropping and Y's Exchanging words.

Suffixes								
-able	*-al*	*-er*	*-ical*	*-ism*	*-ist*	*-ment*	*-ness*	*-ous*

Spelling Words	Derivatives
publish	publisher, punishable
manufacture	manufacturable, manufacturer
imprison	imprisonable, imprisonment
present	presentable, presenter
breathe	breathable, breather
employ	employable, employer, employment
serve	servable, server
brace	braceable
magnify	magnifier
engage	engagement
journal	journalist, journalism
information	informational
region	regional
period	periodical
courage	courageous
debate	debater, debatable
addition	additional
nerve	nervous
fame	famous
famous	famousness

Teacher Note: Although multiple options are listed for some words, only one *derivative* is necessary for each spelling word.

1. A ***clause*** is a set of words that have a ***subject*** and a ***verb***, but which may or may not make sense by itself.
2. An ***adverbial clause*** acts like an ***adverb***. It "modifies" or gives more information about the main ***verb*** in a sentence.
3. ***Adverbial clauses*** can be recognized because they start with these common ***clause signal words***: *when, while, as, since, if,* and *although.*
4. Use as many of your spelling words from List Q-6 as you can to write sentences that start with an ***adverbial clause***. Use each of the ***adverbial clause signal words*** to start your sentences.
5. Always place a comma at the end of your ***opening adverbial clause*** and before the main part of your sentence.
6. Circle the (***adverbial clause***) and underline your new spelling words.

For example: (Although the towel was wet,) I still dried my hands.

When

While

Since

As

If

Teacher Notes:

1. This is a two-page worksheet. See p. 110 for the second page.
2. This sentence structure will often stretch a young student's language skills. Don't be surprised when he needs help forming sentences that start with the ***adverbial clause*** (the part that is added onto the main clause) and the ***main clause*** (the part that can stand on its own).
3. To teach this sentence pattern,
   a. form the main part of the sentence,
   b. add an ***adverbial clause***,
   c. then move the clause into place so that it starts the sentence, and
   d. be sure to add the comma at the end of the *adverbial clausal opener.*

6. Circle the ***adverbial clause*** and underline your new spelling words.

Although

Bonus: Here are some more ***adverbial clause signal words***. Write three more sentences that start with these. Make sure your ***clause*** has a ***subject*** and a ***verb*** and ends with a ***comma***.

Because

Unless

Until

Teacher Note:
Other common ***clausal starter words*** include *after, before, even if, even though, though,* and *whenever.*

Some of these words can also be used as ***prepositions***. How do you know the difference? A clause has both a ***subject*** and a ***verb***, but a ***prepositional phrase*** is missing the verb.

Clause: Because it was raining, he used his umbrella.
Adv starter S Verb Phrase

Phrase: Because of the rain, he used his umbrella.
Preposition Noun Phrase

1. An ***analogy*** is a comparison between two things.
2. Look at the first pair of words and figure out the relationship between them. Then look at the second set of words which is unfinished. They will share the same relationship as the first two. Can you finish the set?

   Red is to strawberry as yellow is to ___lemon or banana___.

   In this example, the comparison (or the relationship) is fruit color.

3. Below are pairs of words. The first pair relate to one another in some way. Use that same relationship to complete the second pair.
4. Use your spelling words from this week's list to complete each set of ***analogies***.

Sun is to sunglasses as rain is to ___umbrella___.

Regress is to backward as progress is to ___forward___.

Ordinary is to important as okay is to ___special___.

Anticipate is to shock as expect is to ___surprise___.

Ocean is to wet as desert is to ___dry___.

Wet is to washcloth as dry is to ___towel___.

Start is to cause as end is to ___result___.

Yes is to maybe as surely is to ___perhaps___.

List Q-6 Alphabetize **ANSWER KEY**

1. As your teacher dictates your spelling words, write them next to the letter that starts that word.
2. Some of your spelling words start with the same letter. As you hear these, write them on the lower part of the page under the appropriate letter. Once you have all of the words that start with that letter, add them to the upper chart in ***alphabetical*** order.
3. When you're done with your quiz, all your words will now be in ***alphabetical*** order.
4. Correct any errors.

Letters	Spelling Words	Letters	Spelling Words
a	although	i	include
b	backward	p	perhaps
d	debit		progress
	debt	r	religion
	dried		result
	dry	s	special
e	effort		surprise
	estate	t	their
	example		towel
f	forward	u	umbrella

Teacher Notes:

1. Read the List Q-6 words ***as they are listed in the WG.*** Your student will select where to write each word and which words need to be written on the lower part of the page first to determine correct *alphabetical* order.
2. The words below are in the order they will be written as you dictate the words. Let him determine that these words should be written here before he adds them to the *alphabetical* chart in the correct order.

d
debt
debit
dry
dried

e
estate
effort
example

s
surprise
special

p
progress
perhaps

r
religion
result

t
towel
their

1. Take a quiz on some of your new spelling words. Correct your work.
2. English grammar includes the eight different ***parts of speech*** listed on page B27 in your Learning Log.
3. A word can fulfill the role of different ***parts of speech***, depending on how it is used in the sentence. The meaning of the word will change depending on how it is being used.
4. Each word you wrote can be used as at least two different ***parts of speech***. Use the dictionary to find out what they are.
5. For each word, add a check (✓) under each column that lists the ***part of speech*** it could be.

Spelling Words	Noun	Adjec-tive	Pro-noun	Verb	Adverb	Prepo-sition	Conjunc-tion	Inter-jection
surprise	✓	✓		✓				✓
progress	✓	✓		✓				
debit	✓			✓				
estate	✓	✓						
towel	✓	✓		✓				
forward	✓	✓		✓	✓			
backward		✓			✓			
special	✓	✓						
dry		✓		✓				
result	✓			✓				

Wise Guide
Enrichment Activity
Worksheets

Lists R-1 to R-6

1. Take a quiz on some review words and some of this week's words.
2. Correct your quiz so that everything is spelled correctly.
3. Use the words in the Word Bank to create ***compound words*** out of your spelling words.
4. If you're using the Bonus Words to make ***compound words,*** all but two of your words can have at least two derivatives. If you're not using the Bonus Words, all but four can have at least two derivatives.

Review Words			Bonus Words
back	hand	pick	bitter
eye	heart	place	brush
fish	leaf	stay	coach
foot	less	ship	wealth

Spelling Words	Compound Words	Compound Words
common	commonplace	**commonwealth**
sword	swordfish	swordplay
stage	backstage	stagehand, **stagecoach**
tooth	eyetooth	toothpick, **toothbrush**
loose	footloose	loose-leaf
sweet	sweetheart	**bittersweet**
wreck	shipwreck	
honor	honorless	

Teacher Note: The optional Bonus Words above are not taught in the WG but can easily be taught now to give your student more of a challenge on vocabulary. Words in **bold** incorporate the Bonus Words.

1. An ***analogy*** is a comparison between two things.
2. Look at the first pair of words and figure out the relationship between them. Then look at the second set of words which is unfinished. They will share the same relationship as the first two. Can you finish the set?

Red is to strawberry as yellow is to banana or lemon.

In this example, the comparison (or the relationship) is the color of a fruit.

3. Below are pairs of words. The first pair relate to one another in some way. Use that same relationship to complete the second pair.
4. Use your spelling words from this week's list to complete each set of ***analogies***.

A teacher has a student; a doctor has a patient.

Loss is to comfort as victory is to congratulate.

Garbage is to worthless as ruby is to precious.

Inspiring good is to encourage as enticing bad is to tempt.

An audience is to seats as an actor is to a stage.

Diamond is to gravel as precious is to common.

A lemon is sour; a pie is sweet.

Bullet is to gun as blade is to sword.

Paper is to wad as car is to wreck.

Cement is to jelly as firm is to loose.

Chef is to bake as scientist is to experiment.

Hand is to finger as gum is to tooth.

1. A ***noun*** is a word that describes a person, a place, a thing, or an idea. You know it's a ***noun*** when you can put ***a, an, the,*** or a number word in front of it.

   an umbrella *the towel* *six examples*

2. Listen as your teacher reads your spelling words to you. What kind of a ***noun*** is it? Write the word in the correct column below.
3. Correct your work.

Person	Place	Thing	Idea
lawyer	shelf	radio	success
prisoner	valley	video	variety
enemy		shelf	eternity
		valley	idea
		mouse	
		echo	
		diamond	
		salary	
		prefix	
		sheep	
		moose	
		piano	
		tomato	

Teacher Notes:

1. Read the words ***in the order they occur in the WG.*** You want your student to have to decide where to write the words.
2. Some words could fit into more than one category. For example, a ***shelf*** can be a ***place*** to put something or a ***thing*** you put on the wall.
3. Allow your student to choose the category that makes sense to him on these kinds of words.
4. An idea is something that exists in the mind and is intangible or cannot be experienced by the five senses.

1. As your teacher dictates your spelling words, write them in their ***plural*** form in the part of the ***Plurals Rule*** they are following.
2. Correct your work to be sure everything is spelled correctly.

To make a word plural, just add an -S:	
valleys	prisoners
diamonds	ideas
lawyers	
UNLESS the word ending hisses:	
prefixes	successes
Changes:	
shelves	eternities
salaries	enemies
varieties	
Ends with O:	
echoes	tomatoes
No change:	
sheep	moose
Internal change:	
mice	
Foreign spelling:	
radios	pianos
videos	

Teacher Notes:

1. Read the words ***in the order they occur in the WG.*** You want your student to have to decide how the Plurals Rule applies to them and where to write the words.
2. Refer to SWR Step #27 for more about the Plurals Rule.

WG p. 165

1. Write the 12 ***adjectives*** and 1 ***noun*** your teacher dictates in the ***Adjectives*** column below. Correct your work.
2. ***Adverbs*** are words that
   a. can be used to modify or describe ***verbs***, ***adjectives***, or other ***adverbs***
   b. can hide in different places in a sentence, but are often before or after the ***verb***
   c. can end with the ***-ly suffix*** but don't always
   d. answer these questions: ***how?*** ***where?*** ***when?*** ***how often?*** ***to what extent?***
3. Write each of these words again with the ***-ly suffix*** in the ***Adverbs*** column. Watch out for any spelling rules that need to be used.
4. Look in your Learning Log List R-3 for two more ***adverbs*** that don't use the ***-ly suffix***. Add them to the ***Adverbs*** column.
5. Finally, in the last column write the question that each of your ***adverbs*** answer (see above).

Adjectives	Adverbs	Question
fierce	fiercely	how
gracious	graciously	how
humble	humbly*	how
bright	brightly	how *or* to what extent
busy	busily	how
general	generally	how
square	squarely	how
according	accordingly	how
angry	angrily	how
secure	securely	how
increasing	increasingly	how often
due	duly**	how
Noun: manner	mannerly	how
	tomorrow	when
	already	when

Teacher Note:
*This is a shortened form of *humble + ly* for ease in speech

**The silent final E is no longer needed; U is not at end of word, and U can say /U/ at the end of a syllable.

1. In order to communicate effectively, a good writer looks for fresh, original comparisons. A ***simile*** is an expression using "as" or "like" in which one thing is compared to another that is well-known.

    The student was as *wise as an owl.*
    The patient was as *sick as a dog.*
    Her cousin was as *proud as a peacock.*
    She sings *like an angel.*
    The kids fought *like cats and dogs.*
    The boy swam *like a fish.*

2. As your teacher dictates your spelling words, write them on the first line for each ***simile***.
3. Correct your work.
4. For each ***simile***, think of something that is typical of the descriptive word you wrote. For example, elephants are known for being big, so we could say, "The house was as big as an elephant."
5. Complete the ***similes*** below with your comparisons.

The cake was as __square__ as ____________________.

The princess was as __humble__ as ____________________.

The maid was as __busy__ as a ____________________.

Mother was as __gracious__ as ____________________.

The chrome shined as __bright__ as ____________________.

The knight was as __fierce__ as ____________________.

The __general__ was as __angry__ as ____________________.

1. Take a quiz on some of this week's spelling words in the first column. Correct your quiz.
2. We add the endings ***-er*** and ***-est*** to adjectives to express comparison.

   My tooth is **loose.** My tooth is **looser** than Mary's. Tom's tooth is the **loosest** of all.

   -er more of — *comparing two*

   -est the most — *comparing three or more*

2. Some multi-syllable words do not change with these suffixes. Instead the adjective stays the same but has *more* or *most* in front of it.

   a *careful* man a *more careful* man a *most careful* man

3. Practice adding the ***-er and -est*** suffixes to each word. Watch out for your spelling rules.
4. Two words from R-1 are completed as examples for you.

Positive Degree Adjectives	**Comparative Degree** Comparing with *-er*	**Superlative Degree** the "most" with *-est*
sweet	sweeter	sweetest
loose	looser	loosest
fierce	fiercer	fiercest
gracious	more gracious	most gracious
humble	more humble	most humble
bright	brighter	brightest
busy	busier	busiest
square	squarer	squarest
angry	angrier	angriest

5. Write a sentences using one of your ***comparative adjectives*** and another one using a ***superlative adjective***. Try to include new or recent spelling words.

Answers will vary.

Examples: Her singing voice was sweeter than honey.

The fierce knight had his busiest week of all by slaying ten dragons.

1. Take a quiz on this week's words in the first column. Correct your work.
2. Add ***prefixes*** to your words to create ***derivatives***.
3. Some words might need a ***suffix*** to create a real word.

Prefixes							
al-	in addition	*im-*	not	*post-*	after, behind	*ultra-*	on the far side of, beyond
dis-	not, opposite	*in-*	not, in	*re-*	again, back, once	*un-*	not

Spelling Words	**Derivatives**
modern	ultramodern, postmodern
popular	unpopular
complete	incomplete
adopt	readopt
revealed	unrevealed
distribute	redistribute
different	indifferent
satisfy	dissatisfy, unsatisfied
control	ultracontrol, uncontrolled
publication	prepublication, republication
search	research
together	altogether
patience	impatience
consider	reconsider, inconsiderate
injure	reinjure, uninjured
injury	post-injury
interest	disinterest, uninterested
education	re-education (some dictionaries omit the hyphen)

Teacher Note: This is a 2-1-1 word. (→ uncontrolled)

1. An ***antonym*** is a word that means the ***opposite*** of something else. or example, *combine & separate* or *lose & find* are ***antonyms***.
2. Read the words in the first column. Which of your spelling words are the ***antonyms***? Write them in the second column.
3. Are there some left that you're not sure about? Listen as your teacher reads your spelling words to you. Write the last ones.

Antonyms	Spelling Words
collect	distribute
disappoint	satisfy
same	different
ancient	modern
conceal	reveal
reject	adopt
ignore	consider
separated	together
heal	injure

4. Write a sentence using one of the ***antonyms*** listed above and then rewrite the sentence using the spelling word that means the ***opposite***. You'll have two sentences with ***opposite*** meanings when you're done. Underline the ***antonyms*** in each sentence.

Answers will vary.

Examples: God chose to conceal the mysteries of Christ in the Old Testament.

God chose to reveal the mysteries of Christ in the New Testament.

1. A ***synonym*** is a word that has a ***similar meaning*** as another word. For example, *release & discharge* and *angry & furious* are ***synonyms***.
2. Read the words in the first column. Do you know what they mean? Can you match them with your spelling words that are the ***synonyms***? Write them in the right column. If you don't know them all, continue to #3.
3. Listen as your teacher reads your spelling words to you slowly. Write the remaining spelling words next to their ***synonyms***.

Synonyms	Spelling Words
forbearance	patience
well liked	popular
uncover	reveal
select	adopt
hurt	injury
unlike	different
contemporary	modern
disperse	distribute
motivation	purpose
total	complete
hunt	search
please	satisfy

4. Write a sentence using one of the ***synonyms*** listed above and then rewrite the sentence using the spelling word that has the ***same meaning***. You'll have two sentences with ***similar*** meanings when you're done. Underline the ***synonyms*** in each sentence.

Answers will vary.

Examples: The building on the corner has a contemporary style.

The building on the corner has a modern style.

1. Take a quiz on this week's words in the first column. Correct your work.
2. Add ***suffixes*** to your words to create one ***derivative*** for each word in the second column.
3. In the third column write the rule you had to use to create the ***derivative*** (E's Dropping, 1-1-1, or 2-1-1). If can just add the ending without using any rules, leave that line in the third column blank.

Suffixes											
-able	*-ed*	*-en*	*-ful*	*-ible*	*-ing*	*-ist*	*-ive*	*-ly*	*-ment*	*-ous*	*-y*

Spelling Words	Derivatives	Rule
choose	choosing, choosy	E's Dropping
entertain	entertained, -entertaining, -ment	
weigh	weighable, weighed, weighing	
improve	improvable, -ed, -ing // improvement	E's Dropping // Word + ending
promise	promised, promising	E's Dropping
prefer	preferred, preferring, preferable*	2-1-1
chose	chosen	E's Dropping
illustrate	illustrated, illustrating, illustrative	E's Dropping
prepare	prepared, preparing	E's Dropping
soldier	soldiered, soldiering, soldierly	
machine	machinist	E's Dropping
treason	treasonable, treasonous	
objection	objectionable	
service	serviced, servicing, serviceable**	E's Dropping
treasure	treasured, treasuring, treasury	E's Dropping
create	created, creating, creative	E's Dropping
creation	creationist	
quiz	quizzed, quizzing	1-1-1
effect	effected, effectible, effective	

Teacher Notes:
*The accent shift causes this word to not fit the 2-1-1 Rule.

**Rule 2 overrides Rule 16 (see SWR pg 147).

Although multiple options are provided, the student only needs to write one *derivative* per spelling word.

1. A ***synonym*** is a word that has a ***similar meaning*** as another word. For example, *complete & thorough* and *injure & wound* are ***synonyms***.
2. Read the words in the first column. Do you know what they mean? Can you match them with your spelling words that are the ***synonyms***? Write them in the right column. If you don't know them all, continue to #3.
3. Listen as your teacher reads your spelling words to you slowly. Write the remaining spelling words next to their ***synonyms***.

Synonyms	Spelling Words
test	quiz
prize	treasure
select	choose
draw	illustrate
assistance	service
amuse	entertain
better	improve
design	create
pledge	promise

4. Write a sentence using one of the ***synonyms*** listed above and then rewrite the sentence using the spelling word that has the ***same meaning***. You'll have two sentences with ***similar*** meanings when you're done. Underline the ***synonyms*** in each sentence.

Answers will vary.

Examples: I will always do better when I study.

I will always improve when I study.

1. A ***clause*** is a set of words that have a ***subject*** and a ***verb***, but which may or may not make sense by itself.
2. An ***adverbial clause*** acts like an ***adverb***. It "modifies" or gives more information about the main ***verb*** in a sentence.
3. ***Adverbial clauses*** can be recognized because they start with these common ***clause signal words***: *where, when, while, as, since, if,* and *although*.
4. Use as many of your spelling words from List R-6 as you can to write sentences with ***adverbial clauses*** in the middle or at the end of your sentences. Write one sentence using each of the ***adverbial clause signal words***.
5. Circle the ***adverbial clause signal word*** and underline the entire ***adverbial clause***.

For example: More neighbors must pull up their sleeves and help others (if) we are to solve the poverty disaster within a decade.

where

when

while

as

since

Teacher Notes:

1. This is a two-page worksheet. See p. 129 for the second page.
2. This sentence structure will often stretch a young student's language skills. Don't be surprised when he needs help forming sentences that include a ***main clause*** (the part that can stand on its own) with the ***adverbial clause*** (the part that is added onto the main clause).
3. To teach this sentence pattern,
   a. form the main part of the sentence, and
   b. add an ***adverbial clause***.
4. Sometimes you'll need to prompt him to help him finish the idea. For example, Mother put the plates away where....

   ...I could not reach them.
   ...they were safe.
   ...we would find them again.
5. If he has trouble thinking of his own ***adverbial clauses***, suggest several and have him choose one to write.

5. Circle the ***adverbial clause signal word*** and underline the entire ***adverbial clause***.

For example: More neighbors must pull up their sleeves and help others (if) we are to solve the poverty disaster within a decade.

if

although

Bonus: Here are some more ***adverbial clause signal words***. Write three more sentences using these. Make sure your ***clause*** has a ***subject*** and a ***verb***.

because

unless

until

Teacher Note:
Other common ***clausal starter words*** include *after, before, even if, even though, though,* and *whenever.*

Some of these words can also be used as a ***preposition***. How do you know the difference? A clause has both a ***subject*** (S)and a ***verb*** (V), but a ***prepositional phrase*** is missing the ***verb***.

Clause: The janitor cleaned the room (before) he went home.
S V

Phrase: The janitor cleaned the room (before) six o'clock.
Noun

1. English has eight ***parts of speech***. Your spelling words this week represent four of them.

Nouns	persons, places, things, ideas
Adjectives	words that describe nouns
Verbs	action or state of being words
Prepositions	shows a relationship between a noun or pronoun & some other word

2. Take a quiz on your spelling words, but as you write them, choose which ***part of speech*** the word would fit into, including the kind of ***nouns***.
3. Correct your work to make sure everything is spelled correctly.

Nouns			
Persons	**Places**	**Things**	**Ideas**
neighbor	vessel	sleeve	feature
visitor	avenue	pickle	poverty
janitor		tobacco	advice
		article	decade
		liquid	disaster
			method

Adjectives	**Verbs**	**Prepositions**
beige	drown	toward
		against

Wise Guide Enrichment Activity Worksheets

Lists S-1 to S-6

1. Take a quiz on your spelling words in the 1st column. Correct your work.
2. All of these spelling words can be used as an ***adjective***, a word that describes a ***noun***. By adding the ***suffix -ly*** we can often change an ***adjective*** into an ***adverb,*** a word that describes a ***verb***, an ***adjective***, or another ***adverb***.
3. Write each ***adjective*** as an ***-ly adverb***. Watch for spelling rules that affect how we change the word.

Adjectives	Adverbs
impartial	impartially
particular	particularly
pleasant	pleasantly
serious	seriously
peculiar	peculiarly
fertile	fertilely
constant	constantly
possible	possibly
natural	naturally
grateful	gratefully
local	locally
brilliant	brilliantly
original	originally
anxious	anxiously
total	totally
temporary	temporarily
certain	certainly
opposite	oppositely
divine	divinely
handy	handily

Teacher Notes:

1. We create a double consonant when we add the *-ly* suffix to a base word ends with an L (*impartially, naturally, gratefully,* and *originally*). Does the student notice this pattern?
2. Base words that end with the 4th type of silent final E will drop the E and bring the *-ly* suffix into the final syllable. The Y now fills the role of the required vowel (*possibly*). Other silent final E words simply add the *-ly* suffix (*fertilely, oppositely,* and *divinely*).
3. Can your student explain why the ***adverbs*** *temporarily* and *handily* include the letter I before the *-ly*? (Y's Exchanging Rule)

1. An ***antonym*** is a word that means the ***opposite*** of something else. For example, *toward* & *away from* or *visitor* & *host* are ***antonyms***.
2. Take a quiz on some of your spelling words in the first column. Correct your work.
3. Create an ***antonym*** of as many of your spelling words as possible by simply adding one of the ***prefixes*** meaning "not" (***im-, in-, non-, and un-***). Use your dictionary to make sure you're using the correct ***prefix*** for each word.

Affirmative	Negative
partial	impartial or nonpartial
grateful	ungrateful
constant	inconstant
particular	nonparticular
pleasant	unpleasant
original	unoriginal
local	nonlocal
certain	uncertain
possible	impossible
fertile	infertile
natural	unnatural

4. Read the words in the first column. Which of your spelling words are the ***antonyms***?

Antonyms	Spelling Words
fake	original or natural
permanent	temporary
calm	anxious
partial	total or impartial
joking	serious
ordinary	brilliant or peculiar
inconvenient	handy

Teacher Note:
Some of the *antonyms* could have two different answers from the spelling list. Your student only needs to supply one answer.

1. Some of your spelling words this week can be used as a ***noun*** or a ***verb***.

   nouns name a person, place, thing, or idea
   verbs describe an action

2. Take a quiz on your spelling words, writing them in the correct columns, depending on whether the word can be used as a ***noun*** or a ***verb***. Two of your words could be both a ***noun*** and a ***verb***, so list them twice.

3. Correct your work to make sure everything is spelled correctly.

Nouns	
century	theater
centennial	megaphone
centimeter	belief
examination	ability
marriage	union
condition	behavior
government	**course**
knowledge	

Verbs
examine
marry
condition
stopped
believe
behave
course

TEACHER NOTES:

1. Dictate the words as a quiz ***in the order they appear on WG p. 178***. Do not give a sentence.
2. Have the student use the word in an oral sentence and decide if it was used as a ***noun*** or a ***verb***.
3. Since he's on the lookout for two words that could be both a ***noun*** and a ***verb***, he should try to use the words both ways in two separate sentences. Could the word be used either way?
   a. If not, then he has to choose the category for how he used the word in his sentence.
   b. If so, then he should list the word in both categories.
4. The words listed above in **bold** are both a ***noun*** and a ***verb***.

1. Take a quiz on Lists S-1 and S-2.
2. Correct your quiz so that everything is spelled correctly.
3. Finish your assignment on the Modifiers - Part 2 worksheet.

List S-1 (Adjectives & Adverbs)	List S-2 (Nouns & Verbs)
impartial	century
possible	centennial
total	centimeter
particular	examine
natural	examination
temporary	marry
pleasant	marriage
grateful	condition
certain	government
serious	stopped
local	knowledge
opposite	theater
peculiar	megaphone
brilliant	belief
divine	believe
fertile	ability
original	union
handy	behave
constant	behavior
anxious	course

1. Use the words you wrote on the Modifiers - Part 1 worksheet to create ________ two-word phrases in which the words from List S-1 ***modify*** the words from List S-2.
2. Mix up the words as you like, but make sure you use your ***modifiers*** appropriately and that each word is only used once.

adjectives	modify	***nouns***
adverbs	modify	***verbs, adjectives,*** and other ***adverbs***

Phrases with Modifiers
Answers will vary.
Examples: *impartial examination*
particular theater

TEACHER NOTES:

1. There is room on this page for 20 phrases. Choose how many phrases you want your student to create and add that number to the line above.
2. If your student has trouble with this assignment, it may be due to his not fully understanding the vocabulary. Make sure he understands the meaning of the words.
3. Walk him through the process of determining which parts of speech each word could be. For example, *century* is a *noun*, so it can only be modified by an *adjective*.
4. Have him try to use the phrases he comes up with in oral sentences. Do they make sense? If not, why not?
5. See WG p. 178 for more possible phrase combinations.

1. Take a quiz on your spelling words in the first column below.
2. Correct your work to be sure everything is spelled correctly.
3. Add ***prefixes*** to your words to create ***derivatives,*** or words that have word parts added to a root word. Each word can have at least one ***derivative***.

Prefixes					
amphi-	around, on both sides	*in-*	in	*re-*	again, once more
bi-	two	*inter-*	between	*super-*	above, over
dis-	not	*mis-*	incorrectly, wrongly	*tri-*	three
fore-	before	*non-*	not	*un-*	not
		pre-	before		

Spelling Words	Derivatives
centennial	bicentennial, tricentennial
examine	re-examine, re-examination
marry	intermarry, remarry, remarriage
condition	precondition, unconditional, recondition
government	misgovernment
stopped	unstopped
knowledge	foreknowledge
theater	ampitheater
belief	unbelief, disbelief
believe	disbelieve
ability	inability, superability, disability
union	reunion, disunion, nonunion
behave	misbehave
behavior	misbehavior
course	discourse, forecourse, recourse

Teacher Note: Although multiple options are listed for some words, only one *derivative* is necessary for each spelling word.

1. Use the clues at the bottom of the page ("Across" and "Down") to fill in the puzzle with new vocabulary words that use the ***bi-*** and ***tri-*** ***prefixes.***
2. If you need help matching the vocabulary words with their clues, you can use a dictionary.

BI-	**TRI-**
bicycle	tricycle
bisect	triangle
bicuspid	tricuspid
biceps	triceps
bifocals	trigraph
bilateral	trimonthly

Across

2. Three letters used to spell a single sound (e.g. igh, dge, tch)
3. A three-headed muscle
4. Every two months
5. Glasses with two different focuses
6. To divide by two
8. Two sides
11. A double-pointed tooth

Down

1. A two-wheeled vehicle
3. Every three months
7. A shape that has three sides and three angles
8. A two-headed muscle
9. A three-pointed tooth
10. A three-wheeled vehicle

1. Write your spelling words as your teacher dictates them.
2. When you're done with your quiz, your words will now be in ***alphabetical*** order!
3. Correct any errors.

Letters	Spelling Words	Letters	Spelling Words
a	ability	h	handy
	anxious	i	impartial
b	behave	k	knowledge
	behavior	l	local
	belief	m	marriage
	believe		marry
	brilliant		megaphone
c	centennial	n	natural
	centimeter	o	opposite
	century		original
	certain	p	particular
	condition		peculiar
	constant		pleasant
	course		possible
d	divine	s	serious
e	examination		stopped
	examine	t	temporary
f	fertile		theater
g	government		total
	grateful	u	union

TEACHER NOTES:

1. Start this activity by giving a quiz on Lists S-1 and S-2, having your student write the words on 3x5 cards. Have him correct any errors.
2. Demonstrate how to alphabetize the words using the cards.
3. Collect the cards once they are in *alphabetical* order.
4. As a final quiz, dictate the words again, having him write them on this worksheet. The result will be an *alphabetized* list of all 40 spelling words.
5. Have him correct any spelling errors.

1. Take a quiz on your spelling words in the first column. Correct your work.
2. Add ***suffixes*** to your words to create ***derivatives***. Which rules will you use to add these endings?
3. All of the words can have at least two ***derivatives***.

Vowel Suffixes				
-aire	*-ary*	*-er*	*-ing*	*-ity*
-al	*-atic*	*-ess*	*-ism*	*-ize*
-ant	*-ed*	*-ic*	*-ist*	*-o*

Consonant Suffixes	
-cy	*-less*
-ful	*-ly*

Spelling Words	Derivatives	Derivatives
doubt	doubter, doubting, doubtless,	doubtful, doubted, doubtfully
motion	motionless, motioned,	motioning
snooze	snoozing, snoozer,	snoozed
crawl	crawled, crawling,	crawler
wound	wounded	wounding
design	designer, designing,	designed
tie	tied	tying
mention	mentioning	mentioned
assist	assisting, assisted,	assistant
nickel	nickled	nickeling
confession	confessional	confessionary
emotion	emotional	emotionalism
moment	momentary, momento,	momentarily
concert	concerto, concerted, concertize,	concerting
sympathy	sympathize	sympathizer
final	finalize, finalist,	finally, finality
system	systematic	systematically
majesty	majestic	majestically
bankrupt	bankruptcy, bankrupted,	bankrupting
million	millionaire	millionairess

TEACHER NOTE: Even though the word *tie* uses the IE phonogram, our rules will dictate how suffixes are added to it. Notice the E is dropped when we add the *ED past tense ending* (*tied*—E's Dropping), and the I has to be exchanged for a Y when adding the *-ing* suffix (*tying* —Y's Exchanging).

TEACHER NOTE: Some words can take more than one suffix. For example, *doubt* becomes *doubtfully* when we add *-ful* & *-ly* and *emotion* becomes *emotionalism* when we add *-al* & *-ism.*

Teacher Note: Although multiple options are listed for some words, only two *derivatives* are necessary for each spelling word.

List S-3 Alphabetizing

ANSWER KEY

1. Write your spelling words as your teacher dictates them.
2. When you're done with your quiz, your words will now be in ***alphabetical*** order!
3. Correct any errors.

Letters	Spelling Words	Letters	Spelling Words
a	assist	m	majesty
b	bankrupt		mention
c	concert		million
	confession		moment
	crawl		motion
d	design	n	nickel
	doubt	s	snooze
e	emotion		sympathy
f	final		system
		t	tie
		w	wound

TEACHER NOTES:

1. Start this activity by giving a quiz on List S-3, having your student write the words on 3x5 cards.
2. Correct any errors.
3. Demonstrate how to alphabetize the words using the cards. All words need to be *alphabetized*, even when they start with the same letter.
4. Collect the cards once they are in *alphabetical* order.
5. As a final quiz, dictate the words again, having him write them on this worksheet. The result will be an *alphabetized* list of all 20 spelling words.
6. Have him correct any spelling errors.

1. As your teacher dictates your spelling words, write them in their ***plural*** form in the part of the ***Plurals Rule*** they are following.
2. Correct your work to be sure everything is spelled correctly.

To make a word plural, just add an -S:	
sleighs	temperatures
affairs	opinions
paragraphs	onions
islands	pistols
ambitions	mushrooms
UNLESS the word ending hisses:	
differences	canvases
recesses	
Changes:	
dictionaries	groceries
communities	yourselves
vanities	
Occasional words have no change:	
celery	gallows

Teacher Notes:

1. Review the Plurals Rule #22 with your student before starting this page.
2. Read the words ***as they are listed in the WG.*** Your student needs to determine
   - which part of the Plurals Rule applies to the word,
   - where to write it on the page, and
   - how to spell the word in its *plural* form.

1. As your teacher dictates your spelling words, write them next to the letter that starts that word.
2. Some of your spelling words start with the same letter. As you hear them, write these words on the lower part of the page under the appropriate letter. Once you have all of the words that start with that letter, add them to the upper chart in ***alphabetical*** order.
3. When you're done with your quiz, all your words will now be in ***alphabetical*** order.
4. Correct any errors.

Letters	Spelling Words	Letters	Spelling Words
a	affair	m	mushroom
	ambition	o	onion
c	canvas		opinion
	celery	p	paragraph
	community		pistol
d	dictionary	r	recess
	difference	s	sleigh
g	gallows	t	temperature
	grocery	v	vanity
i	island	y	yourself

Teacher Notes:

1. Read the List S-4 words ***as they are listed in the WG.*** Your student needs to select where to write each word and which words need to be written on the lower part of the page first to determine correct *alphabetical* order.
2. The words below are in the order they will be written as you dictate the words. Let him determine that these words should be written here before he adds them to the *alphabetical* chart in the correct order.

a
affair
ambition

c
canvas
community
celery

d
difference
dictionary

g
grocery
gallows

o
opinion
onion

p
paragraph
pistol

1. Below you'll find your spelling words in their original form in the first column, their original meaning in the second column, and their ***language of origin*** in the third column. See the code at the bottom of the page.
2. As your teacher reads your words to you, write each word in the 4th column next to its ***etymology***.
3. Correct your work.

Original Word	Original Meaning	Origin	Spelling Words
slee	vehicle mounted on runners for use on ice and snow	Dutch	sleigh
temperatura	a tempering, moderation	L	temperature
differentia	diversity, to set apart	L	difference
vanus	emptiness, aimlessness, falsity	L	vanity
paragraphos	division of text	G	paragraph
grossarius	wholesale dealer	L	grocery
iegland	land associated with water	OE	island
canevas	having the nature of hemp	OF	canvas
opinari	think, judge, suppose	L	opinion
mousseron	moss	F	mushroom
pišť al	tube, pipe, firearm	Czech	pistol
à faire	what one has to do	OF	affair
sélinon	parsley	G	celery
eower + seolf	form of 'you' + one's own person	OE	yourself
ambire	a going around, especially to solicit votes, striving for favor	L	ambition
communitas	society, fellowship, public	L	community
dictionarium	collection of words and phrases	L	dictionary
unio	single large pearl	L	onion
galga or *gealga*	cross	OE	gallows
recessus	a going back, retreat	L	recess

Teacher Notes:
1. Read the words in the order ***as they are listed in the WG.***
2. Your student needs to select where to write each word based on what he can piece together from the meaning and the spelling of the original *root word.*

F = French G = Greek L = Latin OE = Old English OF = Old French

1. In English, the ***subject*** and ***verb*** need to ***agree*** (or match) in ***person*** and in ***number***.
2. If the ***subject*** of a sentence is ***3rd person*** and ***plural***, then the ***subject noun*** has an ***-s*** or ***-es*** added at the end, but the verb has no extra ending.

The dogs	run.
subject	verb

The flies	buzz.
subject	verb

3. Take a quiz on your spelling words.
   a. The first column will be words that can be used as a ***subject*** of a sentence. Write those in the ***plural*** form.
   b. The second column will be words that can be used as a ***verb***. Write those in the ***plural*** form, which means they have no added endings.
4. Correct your quiz to be sure everything is spelled correctly.

Plural Subjects	Matching Verbs
elephants	frighten
sergeants	acknowledge
companions	purchase
afflictions	accuse
audiences	pressure
musicians	arrive
nieces	affect
bachelors	listen
colleges	investigate
societies	supply

Reminder:
1st person is the person talking or writing.
2nd person is the person being talked to.
3rd person is a person, place, thing, or idea being talked about.

For example: I (*1st person*) will write to you (*2nd person*) about Grandma (*3rd person*).

1. In English, the ***subject*** and ***verb*** need to ***agree*** (or match) in ***person*** and in ***number***.
2. If the subject of a sentence is ***3rd person*** and ***singular***, then the ***singular verb*** has an ***-s*** or ***-es*** added at the end, the same way we create a ***plural noun***.

The dog	runs.
subject	verb

The fly	buzzes.
subject	verb

3. Take a quiz on your spelling words.
   a. The first column will be words that can be used as a ***subject*** of a sentence. Write those in the ***singular*** form.
   b. The second column will be words that can be used as a ***verb***. Write those in the ***singular*** form (with the ***-s*** or ***-es***) on the same line. Watch out for the Y's Exchanging Rule.
4. Correct your quiz to be sure everything is spelled correctly.

Singular Subjects	Matching Verbs
elephant	frightens
sergeant	acknowledges
companion	purchases
affliction	accuses
audience	pressures
musician	arrives
niece	affects
bachelor	listens
college	investigates
society	supplies

Reminder:
1st person is the person talking or writing.
2nd person is the person being talked to.
3rd person is a person, place, thing, or idea being talked about.

For example: I (*1st person*) will write to you (*2nd person*) about Grandma (*3rd person*).

1. Take a quiz on some review words and some of your new spelling words.
2. Correct your quiz so that everything is spelled correctly.
3. Combine your review words with your spelling words to create a ***compound word*** for each spelling word.

Review Words			
apple	beef	buck	cross
eye	head	master	more
pan	some	time	times
	under	work	

Spelling Words	Compound Words
peace	peacetime
quarrel	quarrelsome
further	furthermore
teeth	eyeteeth, buckteeth
piece	crosspiece, eyepiece, headpiece, masterpiece, piecemeal, piecework
steak	beefsteak
often	oftentimes
carriage	undercarriage
sauce	applesauce, saucepan
witness	eyewitness

Teacher Note: Although multiple options are listed for some words, only one *compound word* is necessary for each spelling word.

4. Write a sentence using one of your new ***compound words***.

Answers will vary.

Examples: Oftentimes I will chew on my steak with my teeth neither slowly nor quickly.

Furthermore, he would prefer to take the carriage rather than the motorcar.

1. Take a quiz on your spelling words in the first column. Correct your work.
2. English grammar includes eight ***parts of speech***.
3. A word can fulfill the role of different ***parts of speech***, depending on how it is used in a sentence. The meaning of the word will change depending on which ***part of speech*** it is fulfilling.
4. Look up your words in the dictionary. Put a check mark for each ***part of speech*** each word can be.

Spelling Words	Noun	Adjective	Pronoun	Verb	Adverb	Preposition	Conjunction	Interjection
therefore					✓			
wisdom	✓							
peace	✓							
abundance	✓							
too					✓			
quarrel	✓			✓				
handkerchief	✓							
ceiling	✓							
rein	✓			✓				
neither		✓	✓				✓	
further		✓		✓	✓			
teeth	✓							
piece	✓							
steak	✓							
often		✓			✓			
morsel	✓			✓				
oxygen	✓							
carriage	✓							
sauce	✓							
witness	✓			✓				

1. An ***antonym*** is a word that means the ***opposite*** of something else. For example, *listen* & *ignore* or *arrive* & *depart* are ***antonyms***.
2. Read the words in the first column. These are ***antonyms*** to some of your spelling words. Write your spelling words across from their ***antonyms***. If you don't know them all, continue to #3.
3. Listen as your teacher slowly reads your spelling words. Finish connecting your spelling words to their ***antonyms***.

Antonyms	Spelling Words
ignorance	wisdom
big portion	morsel or piece
carbon dioxide	oxygen
floor	ceiling
rarely	often
war	peace
agree	quarrel
scarcity	abundance
whole	piece or morsel

Teacher Notes: Either of these spelling words is an appropriate *antonym* for the word provided. Have the student choose a different word each time so he's getting practice with more vocabulary words and so he can explore more vocabulary options.

4. Write a sentence using one of the ***antonyms*** listed above and then rewrite the sentence using the spelling word that means the ***opposite***. You'll have two sentences with ***opposite*** meanings when you're done. Underline the ***antonyms*** in each sentence.

Answers will vary.

Examples: Chuck took a <u>morsel</u> of the steak for himself.

Chuck took the <u>whole</u> steak for himself.

Wise Guide
Enrichment Activity
Worksheets

Lists T-1 to T-5

1. Take a quiz on this week's words. Correct your work so that everything is spelled correctly.
2. Each of these words can use at least one of the ***consonant suffixes*** listed below to form a ***derivative***. Write one ***derivative*** for each spelling word in the second column.
3. Which spelling rules must be applied in order to add the ***suffix*** correctly?

Consonant Suffixes				
-ful	*-ment*	*-less*	*-ness*	*-ly*

Spelling Words	Derivatives
commence	commencement
crucial	crucially
recent	recently, recentness
severe	severely, severeness
entitle	entitlement
familiar	familiarly
impossible	impossibly
amuse	amusement
accompany	accompaniment
genuine	genuinely
electrical	electrically
straight	straightly, straightness
political	politically
racial	racially
universal	universally
speech	speechless, speechlessly
circular	circularly
argue	argument
real	really, realness
worship	worshipful

Teacher Note: Although multiple options are listed for some words, only one *derivative* is necessary for each spelling word.

1. As your teacher dictates your spelling words, write them next to the letter that starts that word.
2. Some of your spelling words start with the same letter. As you hear these, write them on the lower part of the page under the appropriate letter. Once you have all of the words that start with that letter, add them to the upper chart in ***alphabetical*** order.
3. When you're done with your quiz, all your words will now be in ***alphabetical*** order.
4. Correct any errors.

Letters	Spelling Words	Letters	Spelling Words
a	accompany	i	impossible
	amuse	p	political
	argue	r	racial
c	circular		real
	commence		recent
	crucial	s	severe
e	electrical		speech
	entitle		straight
f	familiar	u	universal
g	genuine	w	worship

Teacher Notes:

1. Read the List T-1 words ***as they are listed in the WG.*** Your student needs to select where to write each word and which words need to be written on the lower part of the page first to determine correct *alphabetical* order.
2. The words below are in the order they will be written as you dictate the words. Let him determine that these words should be written here before he adds them to the *alphabetical* chart in the correct order.

a
amuse
accompany
argue

c
commence
crucial
circular

e
entitle
electrical

r
recent
racial
real

s
severe
straight
speech

1. Good writers play with language to make it interesting for the reader.
2. One technique you can add to your writing is called ***alliteration,*** which is where the ***sound*** of a ***vowel*** or ***consonant*** is repeated, for poetic effect. There are two types of ***alliteration***: ***assonance*** and ***consonance***.

   Assonance occurs when the sound of a ***vowel*** or ***vowel combination*** is repeated.

   She s**ee**s sh**ee**p sl**ee**ping. Do you hear the /E/ sound repeating?

   Consonance is when ***consonant sounds*** are repeated.

   She **sh**outed and **sh**ooed the **sh**eep to the **sh**elter. Do you hear the /sh/ repeating?

3. As your teacher reads your spelling words, listen to the first ***sound*** of the word. Does it start with one of the ***sounds*** below? If so, write it in a box in that row.

   Note: The letter inside the ***slashes*** indicates a ***sound***. Different letters can spell a ***sound***, so don't only think of spelling words with the letter inside the ***slashes***. Instead, listen for the ***sounds.***

Assonance				
/a/	amuse	accompany		
/e/	electrical	entitle		

Consonance				
/k/	commence	crucial		
/r/	recent	racial	real	
/s/	severe	speech	straight	circular

Teacher Notes:
1. Read all the words from List T-1, ***in the order they occur in the WG***, having your student listen for and record the words that start with these ***sounds.***
2. Continue this exercise by having your student write *allit-eration* sentences on p. 155.

1. Write four sentences that include ***alliteration***, using some of the words from the ***Alliterations*** worksheet.
2. Each sentence needs to include at least two of these spelling words, but you're free to add more words to really saturate the sentence with your sound. (Did you hear that consonance?)
3. Underline your new spelling words and be sure each of your sentence makes sense grammatically.

1. Answers will vary.

Example: We shall commence our crucial and complex community plan.

The electrical outlet entitles me to charge my phone for eternity.

2.

3.

4.

1. Take a quiz on some of your spelling words.
2. Correct your work to be sure everything is spelled correctly.
3. Add ***prefixes*** to your spelling words to make ***derivatives***.
4. On one of the spelling words, you'll replace an existing ***prefix*** with one of the ones below to make the new ***derivative***.

Prefixes			
ac-	toward	*re-*	again, back
de-	opposite of	*semi-*	half
dis-	opposite of	*sub-*	further division
inter-	between	*un-*	not

Spelling Words	Derivatives
deceived	undeceived
division	subdivision
accelerate	decelerate
source	resource
pierced	unpierced, repierced
circle	semicircle
appearance	disappearance, reappearance
national	international

Teacher Notes:

1. The *prefix ac-* is a variation of *ad-* which means "toward." The *derivative* for the spelling word *accelerate* is the opposite, meaning "slow down" or "stop moving toward."
2. Although multiple options are listed for some words, only one *derivative* is necessary for each spelling word.

5. Write a sentence using one of your new ***derivatives***.

Answers will vary.

Examples: We will sit in a semicircle.

The cat's disappearance was a mystery.

1. An ***antonym*** is a word that means the ***opposite*** of something else. For example, *familiar & uncommon* or *argue & agree* are ***antonyms***.
2. Read the words in the first column. Which of your spelling words are the ***antonyms***? Write them in the second column.
3. Are there some left that you're not sure about? Listen as your teacher reads your spelling words to you. Write the last ones.

Antonyms	Spelling Words
multiplication	division
ordinary or normal	weird
huge	minute
disappearance	appearance
international	national
slow	accelerate
presence	absence
straight or with corners	circle
one choice	dilemma
end or result	source
sew up	pierce
be honest	deceived
subordination	reign
local	national
a long time	minute

4. Write a sentence using one of the ***antonyms*** listed above and then rewrite the sentence using the spelling word that means the ***opposite***. You'll have two sentences with ***opposite*** meanings when you're done. Underline the ***antonyms*** in each sentence.

Answers will vary.

Examples: His <u>presence</u> caused a great connection among the group.

His <u>absence</u> caused great division among the group.

1. Some of your spelling words are English ***derivatives*** formed from the ***Greek roots*** listed below.
2. Match your spelling words with their ***roots*** and write them in the last two columns.
3. You will write some words in more than once place.
4. All but three of the ***roots*** can have two ***derivatives***.
5. Can you think of other words that come from these ***Greek roots***? Write **four** of them on the lines below.

Greek Roots	Meanings	Derivatives	Derivatives
auto-	self	autograph	automobile
di-	two	dilemma	division
phon-	sound	telephone	microphone
tele-	far away	television	telephone
mobile	move	automobile	
micro-	small	microphone	
graph-	write	autograph	
video	see	television	division

Other words from these roots:

Possible answers might include...	digraph	microscope	telecast
	dioxide	microscopic	telegraph
autobiography	divide	paragraph	telescope
automatic	microgram	phonograph	telemeter
autonomic	microcosm	phonogram	telephony

1. ***Action verbs*** tell us what the ***subject*** of the sentence did. To be used correctly, they have to match the ***subject*** in certain ways, such as in ***person*** and ***number***.
2. Take a quiz on four sentences. Finish each chart with the different versions of that sentence using the appropriate ***subject pronoun*** and ***present tense verb***.
3. Correct your work to be sure everything is spelled correctly and that your ***verbs*** match the ***subject*** and each other.

Person	Singular	Plural
1st	**I pierce.**	We pierce.
2nd	You pierce.	You pierce.
3rd	(He) pierces.	They pierce.
1st	I deceive.	**We deceive.**
2nd	You deceive.	You deceive.
3rd	(It) deceives.	They deceive.
1st	I reign.	We reign.
2nd	**You reign.**	You reign.
3rd	(She) reigns.	They reign.
1st	I accelerate.	We accelerate.
2nd	You accelerate.	You accelerate.
3rd	(He) accelerates.	**They accelerate.**

Teacher Note: Dictate the sentences in **bold** to your student. He will complete the rest of them.

Teacher Notes:
1. If your student needs help with *pronouns*, see the Subject/Object Pronouns Introduction Worksheet on p. 40. For this *Conjugation* activity, you'll only be using *subject pronouns*.
2. The student can choose which *3rd person singular subject pronoun* (*he, she, it*) he wants to use for each group of sentences. Possibilities are shown above.

1. Take a quiz on some new and review words in the first column. Correct your quiz.
2. The ***suffixes*** below can mean "a person or thing that." In a similar way *man* or *woman* can be used to make ***compound words*** with a similar meaning. A *showman* is "one who shows."
3. Make a ***derivative*** from each of your spelling words that indicates "a person or thing that."
4. Two of your spelling words need to have another ***suffix*** added (*-en* or *-al*) before you can finish with one of the ***suffixes*** listed below.

"a person or thing that..."					
Suffixes				**Base words**	
-er	*-ian*	*-ist*	*-or*	*man*	*woman*

Spelling Words	Derivatives
deceive	deceiver
straight	straightener
accelerate	accelerator
worship	worshiper
real	realist
commence	commencer
minute	minuteman
business	businessman, businesswoman
process	processor, processer
conversation	conversationalist
electric	electrician
bruise	bruiser
discovery	discoverer

1. A ***synonym*** is a word that has a ***similar meaning*** as another word. For example, *crucial & important* and *argue & debate* can be ***synonyms***.
2. Read the words in the first column. Do you know what they mean? Can you match them with your spelling words that are the ***synonyms***? Write them in the right column. If you don't know them all, continue to #3.
3. Listen as your teacher reads your spelling words to you slowly. Write the remaining spelling words next to their ***synonyms***.

Synonyms	Spelling Words
loudness	volume
robber	burglar
religious song	hymn
singing group	choir
pain	ache
company	business
British cookie	biscuit
tummy	stomach
shears	scissors
Easter flower	lily
front-runner	favorite
talk	conversation
a find	discovery
procedure	process
smokestack	chimney
injure	bruise
dryness	drought
refrain	chorus
reward	medal

1. As your teacher dictates your spelling words, write them in their ***plural*** form in the part of the ***Plurals Rule*** they are following.
2. Correct your work to be sure everything is spelled correctly.

To make a word plural, just add an -S:	
biscuits	conversations
stomachs	burglars
chimneys	aches
choirs	electricians
droughts	volumes
medals	hymns
favorites	
UNLESS the word ending hisses:	
businesses	choruses
processes	bruises
Changes:	
lilies	discoveries
Occasional words have no change:	
scissors	

Teacher Note:
Dictate the words ***in the order they occur in the WG.*** The student must decide where on the page to write the word.

3. Write a sentence using one of your new ***plurals***.

Answers will vary.

Examples: Are all businesses closed on Christmas?

The electricians had to work in the burned out building.

1. ***Conjunctions*** are words that connect ***words***, ***phrases***, or ***clauses***. You know and commonly use little ***conjunctions*** such as *and, but, so, or, & yet.*

2. Other ***conjunctions*** work together in ***pairs*** such as *either...or, neither...nor, whether...or, & both... and.* Here are some example sentences using List S words and these ***conjunction pairs***.

   (Either) I will attend the concert, (or) I will take a snooze at home.

   (Neither) Tad (nor) I had a million nickels.

   That particular theater will finally be open on Saturday (whether) I go (or) not.

   (Both) the mushrooms (and) the onions were available at the grocery story.

3. Write _______ sentences using your List T spelling words and the ***conjunction pairs***. Use each ***conjunction pair*** at least once in your sentences. (Circle) each of the ***conjunctions*** in the ***pair*** and bracket them together (see example). Underline your spelling words.

Teacher Notes:

1. Determine how many sentences you want your student to write and fill in the blank for #3.
2. See WG p. 196 for example sentences.
3. Make sure your student uses *both conjunctions* from each pair in a sentence. For example, a sentence using *whether* must also include *or.*

1. Take a quiz on this week's words in the first column. Correct your quiz.
2. Add as many of the ***suffixes*** as possible to your words. Sometimes you can even add two ***suffixes*** to the same word.
3. Two of your words will only have one ***derivative***.
4. Watch for rules that affect how you add ***suffixes*** to the spelling words.

Teacher Note: Although multiple options are listed for some words, only two *derivatives* are necessary for each spelling word.

Suffixes		
-al	*-(e)s*	*-ing*
-ed	*-(i)al*	*-ly*

Spelling Words	Derivatives	Derivatives
compete	competed, competes,	competing
wrestle	wrestled, wrestles,	wrestling
realize	realized, realizes,	realizing
concern	concerned, concerns,	concerning
whistle	whistled, whistles,	whistling
succeed	succeeded, succeeds,	succeeding
forfeit	forfeited, forfeits,	forfeiting
office	official, offices,	officially
exception	exceptional, exceptions,	exceptionally
vary	varied, varies,	varying
various	variously	
ninety	nineties	

5. Write a sentence using one of your new ***derivatives***.

Answers will vary.

Examples: The team forfeited the game because they did not show up on time.

Was he wrestling with a big man or with a big idea?

1. Take a quiz on some spelling words and learn some new words. Correct your quiz.
2. Our phonograms often have their ***roots*** from other languages, and sometimes a phonogram will convey meaning all by itself. For example, words that begin with ***WR*** have a meaning related to ***twisting***. Following are the definitions for this word as both a noun and as a verb.

   Noun - a deviation in direction, curve, bend, turn; the action of turning or rotating on an axis
   Verb - to combine, as two or more strands or threads, by winding together; intertwine

3. Look up each of the words below in a dictionary. Based on what you discover, write in your own words how each of these words relate to the idea of ***twisting***.

Spelling Words		Meaning related to "twisting"
write	**N-1**	twisted lines resulting in letters that convey meaning in words
wrong	**P-7**	deviating from truth or fact; erroneous
wreck	**R-1**	a building or structure that is reduced to a state of ruin
wrestle	**T-4**	wrestlers twist their bodies; we turn thoughts around while wrestling with ideas or problems
wreath	**T-4**	a ring-like, curling formation; twisted branches
wrap		folding or twisting something around something else to enclose it
wrench		to twist suddenly and forcibly; to twist, turn, or move suddenly aside
wrest		to twist or turn; pull, jerk, or force by a violent twist
wring		to twist forcibly; to twist and compress in order to force out water or other liquid
wrinkle		a slight ridge or furrow on a surface due to contraction, folding, crushing, etc.
wrist		the joint between the forearm and the hand that twists and turns

Teacher Notes:
1. Student answers will vary from the definitions listed above. Look for definitions that explain how the words relate to the idea of *twisting,* not just a dictionary definition.
2. The first five words are taught in the Wise Guide Lists indicated above in **bold**. Can your student spell these words without help? Teach the next six words with full spelling dictation, as necessary.

1. Take a quiz on this week's words in the first column. Correct your work.
2. Add ***suffixes*** to your words to create two ***derivatives*** for each spelling word. Sometimes you can use more than one ***suffix*** to form a single ***derivative***.

Suffixes							
-able	*-ally*	*-ation*	*-ed*	*-ence*	*-es*	*-ion*	*-ize*
-al	*-ance*	*-ative*	*-ee*	*-er*	*-ing*	*-ive*	*-y*

Spelling Words	**Derivatives**	**Derivatives**
accident	accidental	accidentally
slip	slipped, slipping, slipper,	slippery
decide	decided	deciding
confer	conferring	conferred
accept	accepted, accepting, acceptable,	acceptance
refer	referred, referring, referral,	*reference,* referee
guess	guessing, guessed, guesses,	guesser
summon	summoner, summoning,	summoned
invite	invited, inviting,	invitation
estimate	estimated, estimating,	estimation
victim	victimize	victimization
medicine	medicinal	medicinally
*conference	*conferencing	*conferences
argument	argumentation	argumentative
product	production	productive
fraction	fractional, fractionally,	fractioned, fractioning

Teacher Note: Although multiple options are listed for some words, only two *derivatives* are necessary for each spelling word.

Teacher Note: *The 2-1-1 Rule will not apply in either of these words because the accent is on the first syllable.

1. Take a quiz on some of your new spelling words or their ***derivatives*** in the first column. Watch out for spelling rules that are needed. Correct your work.
2. Listed below are two ***prefixes*** that can help create ***antonyms,*** or words that mean the ***opposite*** of another word.
3. Note that the meanings of these ***prefixes*** are very similar. Each English word can only take a certain ***prefix*** to create the appropriate ***antonym***. When words can use more than one ***prefix*** to convey a ***negative antonym***, the ***antonyms*** that are created will have subtle differences. That's why it is important to use the correct ***prefix*** to create the new meaning you want.
4. Add a ***prefix*** to each of your spelling words or their ***derivatives*** to create a ***negative antonym***.
5. Use your dictionary to check your answers.

Negative Prefixes	
non-	not, opposite of, lack of
un-	not

Spelling Words	**Negative Antonyms**
accidental	nonaccidental
slippery	nonslipper, unslippery
decided	undecided
conferrable	nonconferrable
acceptable	unacceptable
referred	unreferred
guessable	unguessable
summoned	unsummoned
invited	uninvited
victimized	unvictimized
victimized	unvictimized
productive	unproductive
celebrated	uncelebrated
stationary	nonstationary, unstationary

1. Good writers use ***vivid words***. These are words that are more expressive or more precise. They help the reader understand more clearly what the author is trying to communicate.
2. Take a quiz on some review words and on some of your new spelling words below. Write the words that refer to ***people*** in the first column.
3. In the second column write the words that refer to how someone ***speaks*** to someone else. You will need to make sure your ***verbs*** match their ***subjects*** by adding the appropriate ***suffix*** (***-s or -es***). Do you need to use any spelling rules to add these endings?
4. Correct your quiz to be sure everything is spelled correctly.

Person	Speaks
electrician*	argues*
choir*	worships*
business*	deceives*
folks*	accept
office*	refers
official*	guesses
officer*	summons
wrestler*	invites
victim	estimates
referee	confers

Teacher Notes:

1. ***Dictate these words in pairs*** (e.g. *electrician argue, choir worship,* etc.). ***Do not give the student the 3rd person form of the verbs.*** He must choose to add *-s* or *-es*.
2. These words* are review words or their derivatives from Lists T-1 to T-4.
3. Determine how many sentences you want your student to write and fill in the blank.

5. On a separate piece of paper, use the pairs of words on each line to write ________ sentences with as many of the spelling words from List T-5. For example, you might write: *The electrician argues about the celebration.*
6. Your sentences need to make sense, include proper grammar, and start and end with appropriate punctuation. Make sure your ***subjects*** and ***verbs*** match in number.

Wise Guide
Enrichment Activity
Worksheets

Lists U-1 to U-5

1. Good writers play with language to make it interesting and fun for the reader.
2. One technique you can add to your writing is called ***alliteration,*** which is where a ***sound*** is repeated at the beginning of several words of a sentence. Read this sentence and listen for the ***sound*** that is repeated.

   The cat called for her kittens when they cried for milk.
3. As your teacher reads your spelling words from List U-1, listen to the first ***sound*** of each word. Does it start with one of the ***sounds*** below? If so, write it under the appropriate sound. (The letter inside the slashes indicates a ***sound***, not necessarily the letter at the beginning of the word.)

/b/	/d/	/k/	/s/
beginning	dropped	conserve	survive
bouquet	descend	colony	circumference
	descent	colonies	circumstance
		colonial	science
		colonel	ceremony
		kernels	

Teacher Notes:
1. Read all the words from List U-1, ***in the order they occur in the WG***, having your student listen for and record the words that start with these ***sounds.***
2. Continue this exercise by having your student write *alliteration* sentences on p. 171.

1. Look at your ***Alliterations*** worksheet. Use the two words from the /b/ list to write a sentence. You're free to add more words to really saturate the sentence with your ***sounds***. (Did you hear that ***alliteration***?)
2. Repeat this process with each of the other lists from the worksheet, using at least two words that create ***alliteration*** in each sentence.
3. Write _______ sentences total using other words from List U-1 and other spelling words you've studied that start with the same *sounds*. You can look in your Learning Log for words to use.

Teacher Notes:
1. Determine how many sentences you want your student to write and fill in the blank.
2. See WG p. 202 for more examples of possible sentences.

Answers will vary.

Examples: Father bought me a bouquet for the beginning of my birthday.

Dan descended carefully because the deep descent dropped abruptly.

The concerned colonies needed to conserve kernels of corn.

Sally's science studies helped her sister survive a sad circumstance.

Lists U-1 & U2 Silent Final E Words **ANSWER KEY**

1. Listen as your teacher reads your spelling words from Lists U-1 & U-2.
2. If the word ends with a ***Silent Final E***, write it in the chart below according which type of ***Silent Final E*** it is.
3. One of the ***Silent Final E's*** is not represented in these two lists. Start working your way backwards in your Learning Log and find the first example of that type of ***Silent Final E***. Add it to the chart below.
4. Correct your work so that everything is spelled correctly.

#1	#2	#4
survive	conserve	wrestle or whistle **(List T-4)**
describe	achieve	
penalize	receive	
unfortunate		
revere	**#3**	**#5**
mere	circumference	rehearse
compute	circumstance	response
	science	
	siege	

1. An ***antonym*** is a word that means the ***opposite*** of something else. For example, *forget & remember* or *begin & end* are ***antonyms***.
2. Read the words in the first column. Which of your spelling words are the ***antonyms***? Write them in the second column.
3. Are there some left that you're not sure about? Listen as your teacher reads your spelling words to you. Write the last ones.

Antonyms	Spelling Words
unneeded	necessary
native	foreign
demand	suggest
blessed	unfortunate
reward	penalize
fail	achieve
resist	yield
despise	revere
humility	conceit
depth	height

4. Write a sentence using one of the ***antonyms*** listed above and then rewrite the sentence using the spelling word that means the ***opposite***. You'll have two sentences with ***opposite*** meanings when you're done. Underline the ***antonyms*** in each sentence.

Answers will vary.

Examples: The siege was unneeded since the enemy agreed to surrender at first light.

The siege was necessary since the enemy refused to surrender at first light.

List U-2 Suffixes — ANSWER KEY

1. Take a quiz on your spelling words in the first column. Correct your work.
2. Add the ***suffixes*** below to your words to create ***derivatives***. Sometimes you can add more than one ***suffix*** to a word.

Suffixes							
-able	*-en*	*-er*	*-est*	*-ible*	*-ive*	*-less*	*-ment*
-ed	*-ence*	*-(e)s*	*-ing*	*-ity*	*-ize*	*-ly*	*-ness*

Teacher Note: Although multiple options are listed for some words, only two *derivatives* are necessary for each spelling word.

Spelling Words	Derivatives	Derivatives
yield	yieldable, yielded, yielder, yields,	yielding
siege	sieged, sieges,	sieging
achieve	achieving, achiever, achievable,	achievement, achieved, achieves
receive	receiving, received, receiver,	receivable, receives
conceit	conceited, conceitedly,	conceitedness
vein	veined, veining, veins,	veinless
foreign	foreigner	foreigners
describe	described, describing, describes	describable
response	responseless, responsive,	responsible, responses
rebellious	rebelliousness	rebelliously
neutral	neutrality, neutralize, neutralizer,	neutralized, neutrals
suggest	suggested, suggesting, suggests,	suggestive, suggestible
penalize	penalized, penalizes,	penalizing
unfortunate	unfortunately	unfortunates
revere	revered, revering, reveres,	reverence
mere	merely	merest
height	heighten, heightened, heights,	heightening
necessary	necessarily	necessaries
envelop	enveloping, envelops,	enveloped
compute	computer, computing, computes,	computed, computable

1. As your teacher dictates your spelling words, write them in the ***plural*** form under the part of the ***Plurals Rule*** they are following.
2. Correct your work to be sure everything is spelled correctly.

To make a word plural, just add an -S:	
pigeons	scenes
heirs	journeys
emperors	compliments
citizens	appetites
attorneys	envelopes
customers	vegetables
issues	aisles
tissues	icicles
UNLESS the word ending hisses:	
apparatuses (or just apparatus)	approaches
Changes:	
majorities	difficulties
Occasional words have no change:	
apparatus (or apparatuses)	

Teacher Note: Dictate the words ***in the order they occur in the WG.*** The student must decide where on the page to write the word.

1. The ***articles a*** and ***an*** are used before a ***noun*** or before a word that describes a ***noun***.
2. The ***article a*** is used before a ***consonant sound*** whereas the ***article an*** is used before a ***vowel sound***. Listen carefully to what you're hearing to know which ***article*** to use.
3. To indicate ***ownership*** or ***possession***, we add an ***apostrophe*** and then the ***suffix -s*** to create a ***possessive noun***. The word that follows is what is "owned" or "possessed" by the ***possessive noun***.

   Mary's journey   *an envelope's stamp*   *a grumpy citizen's difficulty*

4. Listen as your teacher reads pairs of words from your spelling list. Write them below with the correct ***article*** and ***possessive*** form. The first one is done for you.

   a colonel's kernel

   a pigeon's journey

   an heir's compliment

   an emperor's appetite

   a citizen's apparatus

   an attorney's envelope

   a customer's vegetable

   a majority's approach

   an issue's difficulty

Teacher Notes:

1. Read the pairs of words above ***without the article*** (e.g. *colonel's kernel, pigeon's journey,* etc.). The student is to decide which *article* to use.
2. Continue this exercise by having your student write sentences showing *possession* on p. 177.

1. Using the word pairs you wrote on the Articles & Possession worksheet, write ________ sentences. Be sure you use the correct ***article*** and ***possessive*** forms.
2. Use any other spelling words from Lists U-1 to U-3 that you are able.
3. Use proper grammar, spelling, and punctuation in each sentence. Underline your Lists U-1 to U-3 spelling words.

Teacher Note:
Determine how many sentences you want your student to write and fill in the blank.

Answers will vary.

Examples: A customer found a colonel's kernel of corn.

The difficulty began when an attorney's envelope turned up missing.

1. A ***synonym*** is a word that has a ***similar meaning*** as another word. For example, *emperor & monarch* and *approach & advance* are ***synonyms***.
2. Read the words in the first column. Do you know what they mean? Can you match them with your spelling words that are the ***synonyms***? Write them in the right column. If you don't know them all, continue to #3.
3. Listen as your teacher reads your spelling words to you slowly. Write the remaining spelling words next to their ***synonyms***.

Synonyms	Spelling Words
tasty	delicious
intricate	elaborate
congressman	senator
greatness	excellence
set apart	distinguish
obtain, get	acquire
intended	meant
divine intervention	providence
lastly	finally
obstruct	interfere
lacking information	ignorance
posh	elegant
secret	confidential
disregard	ignore
cost	expense
essential need	necessity
very old	ancient
obstruction	interference
change	conversion

1. A ***root word*** is the smallest form of a word from which other words are made.
2. Several of your new spelling words are ***derivatives*** of the ***roots*** listed below.
3. As you take a quiz on some of your new spelling words, write each one on the same line as its ***root***.
4. Correct your work.

Root Words	Derivatives
expend	expense
labor	elaborate
ignore	ignorance
interfere	interference
senate	senator
delight	delicious
confident	confidential
distinct	distinguish
mean	meant
converse	conversion
needful	necessity
excel	excellence
provide	providence
final	finally

Teacher Notes:

1. Read the spelling word *derivatives* in the following order:
   senator
   expense
   elaborate
   delicious
   confidential
   conversion
   distinguish
   ignorance
   necessity
   excellence
   meant
   providence
   finally
   interference
2. Allow time in between reading each word so the student can match the *root word* and write the spelling word on the correct line.

5. Write a sentence using one of your new ***derivatives***.

Answers will vary.

Examples: The expense for my trip would be more than I could spend.

I meant to turn right, not left.

1. An ***antonym*** is a word that means the ***opposite*** of something else. For example, *majority* & *minority* or *approach* & *departure* are ***antonyms***.
2. Read the words in the first column. Which of your spelling words are the ***antonyms***? Write them in the second column.
3. Are there some left that you're not sure about? Listen as your teacher reads your spelling words to you. Write the last ones.

Antonyms	Spelling Words
rotten	delicious
house of representatives	senate
luck	providence
inferiority	excellence
public	confidential
luxury	necessity
simple	elaborate
lose, sell	acquire
initially	finally
common	elegant
knowledge	ignorance
modern	ancient

4. Write a sentence using one of the ***antonyms*** listed above and then rewrite the sentence using the spelling word that means the ***opposite***. You'll have two sentences with ***opposite*** meanings when you're done. Underline the ***antonyms*** in each sentence.

Answers will vary.

Examples: His morning meeting was confidential.

His evening meeting was public.

1. As your teacher dictates some of your new spelling words (or the ***root*** of one of your new words), write them in the first column. Correct your work.
2. The words you wrote are ***present tense verbs***. Now write each word again in the second column as a ***past tense verb***. What spelling rules do you need to use to make this change?
3. Which phonogram ***sound*** or ***sounds*** did your ***ED ending*** say? In the last column write the ***sound*** or ***sounds*** the ***ED phonogram*** says in the ***past tense verb***.

   ed ***d*** ***t***

4. Correct your work to be sure everything is spelled correctly.

Present Tense Verbs	Past Tense Verbs	ED Sound
communicate	communicated	ed
reverence	reverenced	d
calculate	calculated	ed
admit	admitted	ed
occupy	occupied	d
respect	respected	ed
develop	developed	t
agree	agreed	d
consider	considered	d
assure	assured	d
divide	divided	ed
conceal	concealed	d

Teacher Note: This is the *root* of *admittance,* one of the new spelling words.

Teacher Note: When a word ends with the double ***ee***, you'll drop one of the E's when adding a suffix that starts with an ***E*** (ed).

5. Write a sentence using one of these new ***past tense verbs***.

Answers will vary.

Examples: I carefully calculated the time it would take me to get to your house.

He agreed to meet me at seven o'clock.

1. Take a quiz on your spelling words. Correct your work.
2. Add ***prefixes*** to your each of your spelling words to make ***derivatives***.

Prefixes											
anti-	*dis-*	*ex-*	*im-*	*ir-*	*mis-*	*ir-*	*pre-*	*re-*	*sub-*	*tele-*	*un-*

Spelling Words	Derivatives
social	antisocial, unsocial
communicate	excommunicate, miscommunicate, recommunicate
reverence	irreverence
probably	improbably
calculate	miscalculate, recalculate, recalculate
application	misapplication , preapplication, reapplication
admittance	preadmittance, readmittance
occupy	preoccupy, reoccupy, unoccupy
material	immaterial
relief	unrelief
courtesy	discourtesy
respectful	disrespectful, unrespectful
developed	undeveloped, predeveloped, redeveloped, misdeveloped
responsible	irresponsible
agreement	disagreement, preagreement
consideration	reconsideration, preconsideration
assured	reassured
vision	television, revision
divided	undivided, redivided
concealed	preconcealed, unconcealed

Teacher Note: Although multiple options are listed for some words, only one *derivative* is necessary for each spelling word.

1. Take a quiz on this week's words in the first column below.
2. Correct your quiz so that everything is spelled correctly.
3. Add ***suffixes*** to your spelling words to make two ***derivatives*** for each spelling word.

Suffixes			
-ary	*-ism*	*-ly*	*-s*
-ed	*-ist*	*-ment*	*-tion*
-ing	*-ize*	*-ness*	*-y*

Teacher Notes: Multiple options are shown, but the student only needs to provide two *derivatives* for each spelling word.

Spelling Words	Derivatives	Derivatives
social	socialism, socialist, socialize,	socially, socials
communicate	communicated, communicating,	communication, communicates
reverence	reverenced, reverences,	reverencing
calculate	calculated, calculated, calculation,	calculating, calculates
occupy	occupied	occupying
material	materialism, materialist, materials,	materialize, materially
respectful	respectfully	respectfulness
responsible	responsibleness	responsibly
assured	assuredly, assuring,	assured, assuredness
vision	visionary	visions
conceal	concealed, concealing, conceals,	concealment

4. Write a sentence using one of your new ***derivatives***.

Answers will vary.

Examples: We had a lot of fun communicating silently.

I respectfully decline your invitation.

1. Look at the words you created on the ***Prefixes*** and the ***Suffixes*** worksheets.
2. Mix and match the ***derivatives*** you made with the ***prefixes*** and ***suffixes*** to create new ***derivatives***.

antisocially	preconcealment
unsocially	preconsiderations
disrespectfully	preoccupied
disrespectfulness	preoccupying
dividedly	prerevision
dividedness	reassuredly
excommunicated	reassuringly
excommunicating	recalculated
excommunication	recalculating
irresponsibly	recalculation
miscalculated	reoccupied
miscalculating	reoccupying
miscalculation	revisionary
miscommunicated	revisionist
miscommunicating	uncalculated
miscommunication	uncommunicated
precalculated	uncommuniating
precalculating	unconcealed
precalucation	unconcealing
preconcealed	undividedly
preconcealing	unoccupied

Teacher Note: While there are 42 options listed here, there is room on the student page for him to create up to 24 *derivatives*.

Wise Guide
Enrichment Activity
Worksheets

Lists V to Z

1. ***Single nouns*** can show ***possession*** by adding an ***apostrophe*** + ***-s***.

   Tom**'s** cat the child**'s** toy Mother**'s** book

2. ***Plural nouns*** show ***possession*** by simply adding the ***apostrophe*** after the ***plural*** ending.

   the pigeon**s'** seed the customer**s'** issues

3. The object being ***possessed*** may or may not be ***plural***, depending on whether the ***nouns*** share ownership of the ***possessed*** item or items.

   the pigeons' seed - more than one pigeon owns the seed
   the customers' issues - each of a group of customers has an issue
   OR a group of customers share more than one issue

4. Using your List V-1 words, create ten ***single possessive noun*** pairs.
5. Finally, use different combinations of List V-1 words to form ten ***plural possessive noun*** pairs.
6. An example is provided below for each.

Teacher Note: Student answers will vary. Examples are provided.

Single Nouns	Plural Nouns
principal's principle	volunteers' licenses
secretary's spaghetti	pianists' secretaries
missionary's cereal	principals' grievances
surgeon's yacht	secretaries' mansions
volunteer's career	missionaries' licenses
association's pianist	surgeons' superstitions

1. ***Nouns*** can fall into four categories: persons, places, things, or ideas.
2. Take a quiz on this week's words, which are all ***nouns***. Write each word in the correct category.
3. Correct your work to be sure all the words are spelled correctly.

Person	Thing
principal	cereal
volunteer	mosquito
missionary	artillery
surgeon	spaghetti
pianist	(association)
secretary	(career)
	(license)
	(yacht)

Place	Idea
prairie	grievance
mansion	principle
berth	superstition
(yacht)	(license)
	(career)
	(association)

Teacher Note: Usually we relegate intangible *nouns* to the category of "ideas." The words *career* and *association* would be "ideas," since they are intangible. The word *license* could be tangible if referring to a piece of paper (marriage license), but it could also be intangible if referring to the authority or permission to do or own something. For example, the police have the license to arrest us. Also, there are *nouns* that could be a place or a thing, such as a *yacht.* It's a "place" to spend the weekend or a "thing" you could buy. Allow your student to wrestle with these *nouns* and make a decision as to how he wants to categorize them.

1. ***Nouns*** can be ***singular*** (one) or ***plural*** (more than one).
2. Take a quiz on this week's words, but write them in their ***plural*** form.
3. Write each word in the correct place, depending on what part of the ***Plurals Rule*** you are applying.
4. Correct your work to be sure all the words are spelled correctly.

Just add -s	**Add -es**
cereals	**... if the word hisses**
principals	licenses*
prairies	grievances*
careers	**... changes**
volunteers	missionaries
associations	secretaries
yachts	**... ends with -o**
mansions	mosquitoes
surgeons	
licenses*	**No change**
pianists	artillery
grievances*	spaghetti
berths	
principles	
superstitions	

Teacher Notes:

1. Read the words ***in the order they occur in the Wise Guide*** so that the student has to decide where to write each word.
2. *The words *license* and *grievance* already end with an E, so all we're really doing to make these words plural is adding the suffix *-s.* However, since these words end with a hissing *sound,* your student might want to add them to the category "...if the word hisses." Let your student decide which category he wants to use. Although they are listed in both pages on this Answer Key, your student will only write them in one place.

1. Take a quiz on this week's words in the first column. Correct your work.
2. Add ***suffixes*** to your words. Which rules do you need to use to add the endings?
3. Look your ***derivatives*** up in the dictionary to be sure they are legitimate English words.

Suffixes						
-able	*-ary*	*-ed*	*-ial*	*-ism*	*-ive*	*-ness*
-age	*-ation*	*-er*	*-ing*	*-ist*	*-ize*	*-or*
-al	*-ative*	*-ery*	*-ion*	*-ity*	*-ly*	*-y*

Spelling Words	Derivatives
mysterious	mysteriously, mysteriousness
relieve	relieved, relieving, reliever
advise	advising, advised, advisable, advisor (-er is also acceptable)
solemn	solemnly, solemnness, solemnity
apparent	apparently
image	imaging, imaged
imagine	imaginative, imaginary, imagination, imagined
column	columnist, columned
independent	independently
evidence	evidenced, evidencing
testimony	testimonial
individual	individualism, individualist, individuality, individualize
sacrifice	sacrificing, sacrificed, sacrificial
prejudice	prejudiced, prejudicial
coarse	coarsely, coarseness, coarser
leisure	leisurely
reference	referenced, referencing, referencial
occasion	occasional, occasionally
acre	acreage **(NOTE: Rule 7 overrides Rule 16)**

Teacher Note: Although multiple options are listed for some words, only one *derivative* is necessary for each spelling word.

1. An ***antonym*** is a word that means the opposite of something else. For example, *surgeon* & *patient* or *career* & *avocation* are ***antonyms***.
2. Read the words in the first column. Which of your spelling words are the ***antonyms***? Write them in the second column.
3. Are there some left that you're not sure about? Listen as your teacher reads your spelling words to you. Write the last ones.

Antonyms	Spelling Words
guilt	innocence
open mind	prejudice
dependent	independent
work	leisure
silky	coarse
see	imagine
obscure	apparent
group	individual
predictable	mysterious
jovial	solemn
burden	relieve

4. Write a sentence using one of the ***antonyms*** listed above and then rewrite the sentence using the spelling word that means the ***opposite***. You'll have two sentences with ***opposite*** meanings when you're done. Underline the ***antonyms*** in each sentence.

Answers will vary.

Examples: The group had a mysterious event planned.

The individual had a predictable event planned.

1. Take a quiz on some of your spelling words. Correct your work.
2. Add ***prefixes*** to your spelling words to make ***derivatives***. Including a ***suffix*** with some of your words helps you make create even more ***derivatives***.

Prefixes					
counter-	*in-*	*non-*	*over-*	*re-*	*un-*
dis-	*mis-*	*ob-*	*pre-*	*sub-*	*under-*

Spelling Words	Derivatives
weight	counterweight, overweight, underweight
campaign	precampaign, recampaign, uncampaigning
consciousness	subsconsciousness, unconsciousness, underconsciousness
controllable	uncontrollable, noncontrollable
organize	reorganize, overorganize, disorganize, misorganize
organization	disorganization, reorganization, overorganization
sense	nonsense
sensible	insensible, nonsensible
compression	precompression, noncompression, overcompression
experience	inexperience
permitted	unpermitted, nonpermitted
profit	nonprofit, unprofitable
arrangement	rearrangement, prearrangement, disarrangement
discussion	prediscussion, rediscussion
session	obsession, presession
welfare	prewelfare
tying	retying, overtying, undertying
resemblance	nonresemblance

Teacher Note: Although multiple options are listed for some words, only one *derivative* is necessary for each spelling word.

1. In the first column take a quiz on some of your new spelling words and some of the roots of your new words. Correct your work.
2. In the second column write the ***part(s) of speech*** each of these words can be used for, using the following codes. **N**oun **ADJ**ective **V**erb
3. Look at the ***parts of speech*** listed in the third column. Add one of the ***suffix endings*** listed below to create a ***derivative*** that fits that ***part of speech*** and write it in the fourth column.

Adjective Suffixes		
-able	*-ible*	*-ous*
-ent	*-ic*	*-y*

Noun Suffixes		
-ance	*-ice*	*-sion*
-ence	*-ness*	*-tion*

Root Words	Part(s) of Speech	Part of Speech	Derivatives
mystery	N	ADJ	mysterious
depend	V	N	dependent
prejudge	V	N	prejudice
refer	V	N	reference
weight	N	ADJ	weighty
conscious	ADJ	N	consciousness
control	V	ADJ	controllable
organize	V	N	organization
sense	N, V	ADJ	sensible
compress	N, V	N	compression
profit	N, V	ADJ	profitable
arrange	V	N	arrangement
discuss	V	N	discussion
resemble	V	N	resemblance
magnify	V	ADJ	magnificent

1. ***Magnus*** is a ***Latin root*** meaning *big, great,* or *large.*
2. We do not use this word on its own in English, but we do see it partly embedded within English words.
3. Look up the definition of each of these words in your dictionary and write the definitions in the second column, keeping in mind the original meeting of ***magnus***.

Teacher Note: The wording for the definitions will vary, depending on your student's dictionary.

***Magnus* derivatives**	**Definition**
magnify	make something appear larger; extol; glorify
magnifier	a person or a thing that magnifies
magnificent	making a splendid appearance or show; extraordinarily fine; superb; noble; sublime
magnitude	size; extent; dimensions; great importance or consequence; greatness of size or amount
magnanimous	generous in forgiving an insult or injury; free from petty resentfulness or vindictiveness; high-minded; noble
magnate	a person of eminence or distinction in any field

1. Take a quiz on some of your spelling words in the first column. Correct your work.
2. In the second column write the ***part of speech*** each of these words can be used for, using the following codes.
   Noun **ADJ**ective **V**erb
3. A ***derivative*** is a word that is made from a ***base*** word. Write the ***base word*** for each of your spelling words in the third column. If you're not sure what it is, look it up in the dictionary.
4. Did the ***part of speech*** change? Write the new ***part of speech*** in the last column.
5. Sometimes a word can fill the role of more than one ***part of speech***. Be sure to include each case.

Spelling Words/Derivatives	Part of Speech	Base Words	Part(s) of Speech
weight	N	weigh	V
organization	N	organize	V
permitted	V	permit	V, N
discussion	N	discuss	V
magnificent	ADJ	magnify	V
consciousness	N	conscious	ADJ
sensible	ADJ	sense	N, V
profited	V	profit	V, N
resemblance	N	resemble	V
controllable	ADJ	control	V, N
compression	N	compress	V, N
arrangement	N	arrange	V
tying	V	tie	V, N

1. There are times when a ***noun*** is immediately followed by another ***noun*** or a ***noun*** with ***modifiers***. When this second ***noun*** renames or further identifies the first ***noun***, it is called an ***appositive***. Together this ***noun*** and any of its ***modifiers*** are called an ***appositive phrase.***

   The little boy played with the toy, <u>the big yellow truck</u>. ***appositive phrase***

2. ***Commas*** are used on either side of an ***appositive phrase*** that has more than one word.

   My teachers, <u>Mr. Harrison and Mrs. Phillips</u>, were the highlight of my high school years.

3. When a short proper name is used to identify the one being discussed, no ***commas*** are needed to set it apart from the rest of the sentence.

   Patty picked up her friend <u>Janet</u> on the way to the concert.

4. Write the sentences your teacher dictates to you below. Use proper punctuation, and <u>underline</u> the ***appositive*** or the ***appositive phrase*** in each sentence.

5. **On separate paper**, write each sentence a second time—this time without the ***appositive***. When you're done, each sentence will be written twice; once ***with*** the ***appositive phrase*** and then again ***without*** the ***appositive phrase***.

Teacher Note: Dictate the ***first sentence shown in*** **bold** in each of these pairs. The *appositive phrases* are underlined. On his own, the student is then to write the sentence *a second time* ***without*** the phrase.

1a. **Our newest vehicle, <u>the jeep</u>, had a flat tire.**

1b. Our newest vehicle had a flat tire.

2a. **The jeep, <u>our newest vehicle</u>, had a flat tire.**

2b. The jeep had a flat tire.

3a. **The Isthmus of Panama, <u>the site of the famous Panama Canal</u>, connects which two oceans?**

3b. The Isthmus of Panama connects which two oceans?

4a. **Using a calculator, <u>an instrument for calculating numbers</u>, makes math easier.**

4b. Using a calculator makes math easier.

5a. **Robert E. Lee, <u>a general in the War between the States</u>, was called a friend without treachery.**

5b. Robert E. Lee was called a friend without treachery.

6a. **Daisy, <u>our heifer</u>, had a sudden emergency.**

6b. Daisy had a sudden emergency.

7a. **My parents' wedding anniversary, <u>July first</u>, is a very special day.**

7b. My parents' wedding anniversary is a very special day.

1. In the first column below you will find some ***Greek and Latin roots***. Some are common ***prefixes*** we use in English. The second column lists the meanings of these ***roots***.
2. Write your spelling words on the line in the third column that matches their ***roots***. Two of your words will be written twice each.
3. Locate which of these ***roots*** are listed on pages B35 & B36 in your Learning Log. Add the spelling words that match those ***roots*** to those pages. **NOTE:** Sometimes only part of the ***root*** is shown on the these pages. For examples, ***ann*** is listed on page B35 for ***annus***.
4. Correct your work so everything is spelled correctly.

Greek & Latin Roots	Root Meanings	Spelling Words	
annus	year	anniversary	**B35 *ann***
athlon	prize	athlete	
facere	make	confectionery	
com-	up, with, together	confectionery	
contro-	against	controversy	**B35 *vers***
kalendarium	account book	calendar	
liber	books	library	
multi-	many	multitude	**B36 *multi***
plicare	fold	employee	
vehere	carry	vehicle	
vertere	turn	controversy	

Teacher Note:
The *roots* and the Black Log Reference Pages where the roots are located are listed in **bold** above.

1. Using the words from the Word Bank at the bottom of the page, complete the crossword puzzle.
2. All of the words have the ***Latin root annus***.
3. Use a dictionary if necessary.

Down
1. events recorded by year
3. every thousand years
5. money paid yearly

Across
2. a plant that lives for more than two years; through the years
4. every two years
6. every hundred years
7. every year

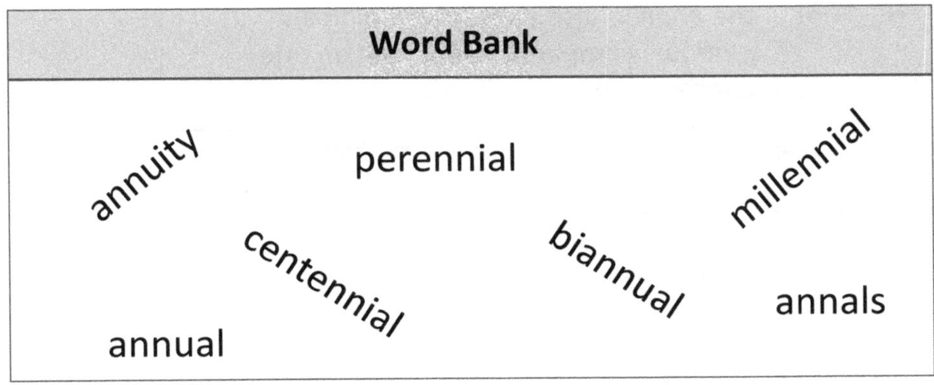

1. Use ***commas*** to punctuate a ***series*** of three or more ***nouns*** or ***verbs***. Include a ***comma*** before your last ***conjunction***.

   We visited Mt. Rushmore, Niagara Falls, and the Grand Canyon. (***noun series***)

   The soccer players dribbled the ball, guarded their goal, and won the game. (***verb series***)

2. Use a ***comma*** to punctuate a ***series*** of two or more ***adjectives*** IF the ***adjectives*** are describing a ***noun*** in two separate ways; the first ***adjective*** can't be describing the second one with the ***noun***.

   I saw the shining, glorious tree. — *Shining* and *glorious* are both describing the tree, so a comma is necessary.

   That is a big bad wolf. — *Big* is describing *bad wolf*, so no comma is used.

3. Take dictation on sentences using W-1 and W-2 words. Make sure you use proper punctuation.

Teacher Notes:

1. See WG p. 222 for sentences to dictate.
2. Clearly pause where the commas belong so the student can get a feel for the natural pause a *comma* communicates.
3. For an *adjective series,* if you could add "and" in place of the commas, then you know the commas are necessary.

   I saw the shining AND *glorious tree.*
   I saw the shining, glorious tree.

   That is a big ~~AND~~ bad wolf.
   That is a big bad wolf.

   The issue is whether the *adjectives* describe the *noun* in distinct ways (*shining* and *glorious*) compared to building on one another to describe it (*big bad*).

1. Take a quiz on this week's words in the first column. Correct your quiz.
2. Add ***suffixes*** to your words to form ***derivatives***. You can use more than one ***suffix*** on some words.

Suffixes								
-ance	*-er*	*-ing*	*-ism*	*-istic*	*-ize*	*-ly*	*-or*	*-ure*
-ed	*-ful*	*-ion*	*-ist*	*-ity*	*-less*	*-ness*	*-s*	*-y*

Teacher Note: Although multiple options are listed for some words, only two *derivatives* are necessary for each spelling word.

Spelling Word	Derivative	Derivative
appreciate	appreciation, appreciated,	appreciating, appreciates
cordial	cordially, cordiality,	cordials
sincere	sincerely	sincerity
separate	separately, separating, separated,	separation, separator, separates
extreme	extremely, extremeness, extremes,	extremist, extremity
accurate	accurately	accurateness
proceed	proceeding	proceeded
instantaneous	instantaneousness	instantaneously
practical	practically	practicality
artificial	artificially	artificiality
antique	antiquity, antiqued, antiques,	antquing
character	characters, characteristic,	characterize
architect	architecture, architected,	architecting, architects
grease	greasy, greasiness, greased,	greaser, greases
associate	associating, associated,	association, associates
resource	resourceful, resourceless,	resourcelessness, resources
persevere	persevered, persevering,	perseverance, perseveres
opportune	opportunity, opportunist,	opportunism
adequate	adequately	adequateness
rhyme	rhyming, rhymed, rhymes,	rhymer

1. Take a quiz on some of your spelling words.
2. Correct them to make sure everything is spelled correctly.
3. Add ***prefixes*** to your spelling words to make ***derivatives***.
4. Look the words up in your dictionary to make sure they are real words.

Prefixes			
in-	into, on, near, towards	*pre-*	before, prior to
mis-	incorrectly, wrongly	*re-*	back, again
non-	not	*un-*	not, against, opposite

Spelling Words	Derivatives
conceive	misconceive, preconceive
apply	misapply, reapply
reproached	unreproached
destruction	indestruction
development	redevelopment, predevelopment
beneficial	nonbeneficial
contagious	noncontagious

5. Write a sentence using one of your new ***derivatives***.

Answers will vary.

Examples: I had a preconceived notion that you would be here today.

His cough was noncontagious.

1. In the first column below are some ***Greek and Latin roots*** that we use in English as ***prefixes***.
2. Look on pp. B33 & B34 in your Learning Log for the meanings for the first five of these ***roots***. Write those in the second column. Look in the dictionary for the meaning of the last two ***roots*** and add those to the second column also.
3. Can you identify which of your spelling words come from these ***roots***? Write them in the third and fourth columns.
4. Think of or find another word that uses each of these ***prefixes*** that is *not* in your list to write in the last column. Use your dictionary if you need help.
5. The ***prefix aero-*** is the ***root*** to several words in English. Find six of them in your dictionary and write them at the bottom of the page.

Greek & Latin Roots	Root Meanings	Spelling Words	Spelling Words	Another Derivative
mono-	one	monotonous		Answers will vary
bi-	two	bicycle		
tri-	three	triangle		
trans-	across, through	transmitter		
mit-	send	transmitter		
aero	air	aerospace	aerosol	
con-	together, with	conceive	conscience	
		contagious,	concentration	

***aero-* Derivatives**	
aerodynamics, aeromedicine	aerometer
aeronautics, aerobatics	aerogram
aeroplane, aerobics	aeromechanics

Teacher Note: The *aero derivatives* your student lists will depend on the dictionary he uses. Possibilities are included.

1. An ***antonym*** is a word that means the ***opposite*** of something else. For example, *proceed* & *recede* or *persevere* & *discontinue* are ***antonyms***.
2. Read the words in the first column. Which of your spelling words are the ***antonyms***? Write them in the second column.
3. Are there some left that you're not sure about? Listen as your teacher reads your spelling words to you. Write the last ones.

Antonyms	Spelling Words
praised	reproached
remove	apply
descend	ascend
dirtying	rinsing
construction	destruction
noncontagious	contagious
exciting	monotonous
receiver	transmitter
harmful	beneficial
servant	sovereign
dilution	concentration
failure	accomplishment

4. Write a sentence using one of the ***antonyms*** listed above and then rewrite the sentence using the spelling word that means the ***opposite***. You'll have two sentences with ***opposite*** meanings when you're done. Underline the ***antonyms*** in each sentence.

Answers will vary.

Examples: His cold was contagious.

His cold was noncontagious.

List X-1 Prefixes & Suffixes

ANSWER KEY

1. Take a quiz on some of your spelling words. Correct your work.
2. Add ***prefixes*** and/or ***suffixes*** to your spelling words to make ***derivatives***. All but three of your words can make at least two ***derivatives***.

Prefixes	
in-	*sub-*
re-	*un-*

Suffixes							
-al	*-ation*	*-er*	*-eur*	*-ian*	*-ier*	*-ly*	*-tion*
-ally	*-ence*	*-ed*	*-ial*	*-ible*	*-ing*	*-ness*	*-ure*

Spelling Words	Derivatives	Derivatives
finance	financier, financial, financing,	financed
thorough	thoroughly	thoroughness
seize	seized, seizure, seizing,	reseized, unseized
counterfeit	counterfeiting, counterfeited,	counterfeiter
mathematic	mathematician, mathematical,	mathematically
vague	vaguely	vagueness
perceive	perceiving, perceived,	unperceived
immense	immensely	immenseness
digest	digestible, indigestible,	digested, digesting
accommodate	accommodating, accommodated,	accommodation
orchestra	orchestral,	orchestration
committee	subcommittee	
possessed	repossessed	
intelligent	unintelligent, intelligently	intelligence
accuracy	inaccuracy	
approximate	approximately, approximated,	approximation
immediate	unimmediate, immediatley,	unimmediately, immediateness
atrocious	atrociousness,	atrociously
opaque	opaqueness	opaquely
decision	indecision, redecision,	decisional

Teacher Note: Although multiple options are listed for some words, only two *derivatives* are necessary for each spelling word, where possible.

1. An ***antonym*** is a word that means the ***opposite*** of something else. For example, *descend* & *ascend* or *receiver* & *transmitter* are ***antonyms***.
2. Read the words in the first column. Which of your spelling words are the ***antonyms***? Write them in the second column.
3. Are there some left that you're not sure about? Listen as your teacher reads your spelling words to you. Write the last ones.

Antonyms	Spelling Words
genuine	counterfeit
incompletely	thoroughly
defectiveness	accuracy
exact	approximate
small	immense
release	seize
clear	vague
stupid	intelligent
lacked	possessed
overlook	perceive
indecision	decision
transparent	opaque

4. Write a sentence using one of the ***antonyms*** listed above and then rewrite the sentence using the spelling word that means the ***opposite***. You'll have two sentences with ***opposite*** meanings when you're done. Underline the ***antonyms*** in each sentence.

Answers will vary.

Examples: That hundred dollar bill is a genuine item.

That hundred dollar bill is a counterfeit item.

List X-2 Alliteration ANSWER KEY

1. Good writers play with language to make it interesting for the reader.
2. One technique you can add to your writing is called ***alliteration,*** which is where the ***sound*** of a ***vowel*** or ***consonant*** is repeated, for poetic effect. There are two types of ***alliteration***: ***assonance*** and ***consonance***.

   Assonance occurs when the sound of a ***vowel*** or ***vowel combination*** is repeated.

   Sh**e** s**ee**s sh**ee**p sl**ee**ping. Do you hear the /E/ sound repeating?

   Consonance is when ***consonant sounds*** are repeated.

   She **sh**outed and **sh**ooed the **sh**eep to the **sh**elter. Do you hear the /sh/ repeating?

3. As your teacher reads your spelling words, listen to the first ***sound*** of the word. Does it start with one of the ***sounds*** below? If so, write it in a box in that row.

   Note: The letter inside the ***slashes*** indicates a ***sound***. Different letters can spell a ***sound***, so don't only think of spelling words with the letter inside the ***slashes***. Instead, listen for the ***sounds.***

Assonance				
/a/	alliteration	amateur	annual	
/e/	eccentric	especially		

Consonance				
/d/	dessert	desert	disappointed	
/l/	laboratory	leopard		
/p/	pediatrician	preliminary	protein	parliament
/r/	restaurant	receipt		
/s/	superintendent	suspicious		

Teacher Notes:

1. Read all the words from List X-2, ***in the order they occur in the WG***, having your student listen for and record the words that start with these ***sounds.***
2. Continue this exercise by having your student write *allit-eration* sentences on p. 206.

1. Write five sentences that include ***consonance*** and ***assonance***, using words from the ***Alliterations*** worksheet.
2. Each sentence needs to include <u>at least two</u> of these spelling words, but you're free to add more words to really saturate the sentence with your sound. (Did you hear that consonance?)
3. <u>Underline</u> your new spelling words and be sure each of your sentence makes sense grammatically.

1. Answers will vary.

Example: An <u>amateur</u> won the <u>annual</u> <u>alliteration</u> contest.

He was <u>especially</u> <u>eccentric</u> about the employee's extreme behavior.

It was important to retrieve the <u>receipt</u> after dinner at the <u>restaurant</u>.

2.

3.

4.

5.

List X-2 Grammar — Parts of Speech Name ____________________

1. Take a quiz on some of your new spelling words or on the ***roots*** of some of your new words in the second column below. Correct your work.
2. The ***part of speech*** for each of your spelling words is written for you in the first column, using the following code. **ADJ**ective **ADV**erb **N**oun **V**erb
3. When we add ***suffixes*** to words, the ***derivatives*** take on new meanings and will likely change to a different ***part of speech***.
4. Write ***derivatives*** for your words in the fourth column that match the ***part of speech*** indicated in the third column. Refer to the ***suffix*** list below. Some of your ***derivatives*** can use two ***suffixes***.

Adverb Suffix
-ly

Adjective Suffix
-ic

Noun Suffixes						
-atory	*-ence*	*-ent*	*-ian*	*-ion*	*-ment*	*-ness*

Parts of Speech	Spelling Words	Parts of Speech	Derivatives
V		N	
N		N	
N, V		ADJ	
		ADV	
V		N	
N, V		N	
ADJ		ADV	
N, ADJ		ADV	
V		N	
ADJ		N	
		N	
		ADV	
ADJ		N	
		ADV	

1. Each of your spelling words from List X-2 is derived from either ***Latin, French, or Greek***. Read through the ***roots*** and their meanings below.
2. As you take a quiz on your spelling words, match them to their ***roots***. Write the words in the appropriate column and on the correct line. One word is listed twice. Correct your work.

Latin Roots	Meaning	English	English
intendere	direct	superintendent	
litera	letter	alliteration	
prae-	before	preliminary	
labor	work	laboratory	
amator	lover	amateur	
annus	year	annual	millennium
specere	look	suspicious	
deserere	abandon	desert	
venire	come	convenient	
recepta	receive	receipt	
punctum	point	disappoint	
mille	thousand	millennium	

French Roots	Meaning	English	
desservir	clear the table	dessert	
parler	to speak	parliament	
restaurer	to restore	restaurant	

Greek Roots	Meaning	English	
pedi	child	pediatrician	
kentron	center	eccentric	
proteios	of 1st quality	protein	
leon	lion	leopard	

1. Words can serve as different ***parts of speech***, depending on how they're used in a sentence.
2. Study the first chart below that explains the roles of ***nouns***, ***adjectives***, and ***adverbs*** in sentences.
3. Take a quiz on your new spelling words and write them in the correct places on the second chart. If the word can be used at all as a ***noun***—even if it can be used as another ***part of speech*** as well—add it to the ***plural nouns*** columns in its ***plural form***.
4. Correct your quiz to be sure everything is spelled correctly.

Parts of Speech	Job in Sentence	Questions it answers	Other Notes
Noun	names a person, place, thing, or idea	who? what?	can be plural
Adjective	describes or modifies nouns	which one? what kind? how many? whose?	usually before the noun or nouns it modifies
Adverb	describes or modifies verbs, adjectives, or other adverbs	how? when? where? why? to what extent?	commonly ends with *-ly*

Plural Nouns	
restaurants	annuals
superintendents	desserts
pediatricians	deserts
eccentrics	leopards
preliminaries	millenniums or millennia
alliterations	receipts
laboratories	proteins
amateurs	parliaments

Adjectives
disappointed
suspicious
convenient

Adverbs
especially

Teacher Note: Dictate the words to your student ***in the order they appear in the WG*** so that he has to determine where they belong on the page.

List Y-1 Word Etymology - Part 1 **ANSWER KEY**

1. Each of your spelling words from List Y-1 is derived from either ***Latin***, ***French***, ***German***, or ***Greek***. Read through the ***roots*** and their meanings below.
2. As you take a quiz on your new words, match the spelling word to its ***root***. Write the words on the appropriate line. Two words will be written in two places.

Latin Roots	Meaning	English	English
candela	candle	chandelier	
geo	earth	geography	
junctum	join	conjunction	
per-	to the end	persistence	
quaerere	seek	exquisite	

French Roots	Meaning	English	English
meter	measure	kilometer	
mis-	bad	mischief	mischievous
mort	death	mortal	mortician
		mortgage	

German Root	Meaning	English	English
kinder	children	kindergarten	

Greek Root	Meaning	English	English
biblio	book	bibliography	
graph	draw, write	bibliography	geography
para-	beside	parable	parenthesis
		paramedic	parallel
theos	god	atheist	enthusiasm

Teacher Notes:

1. Read all the words from List Y-1, ***in the order they occur in the WG***, having your student match the words with their appropriate *roots.*
2. Continue this exercise by having your student complete the geography portion of this lesson on p. 211.

1. Your List Y-1 spelling words came from four different languages, each spoken in a different part of the world.
2. Find these four countries that contributed words from their languages to English and label them on the map below. For example, Greek came from Greece.
3. Eventually, all of the words ended up in England. Find that country and label it also.
4. Draw arrows from each of the original countries showing the paths the travelers bearing their native languages would have taken on their way to England.

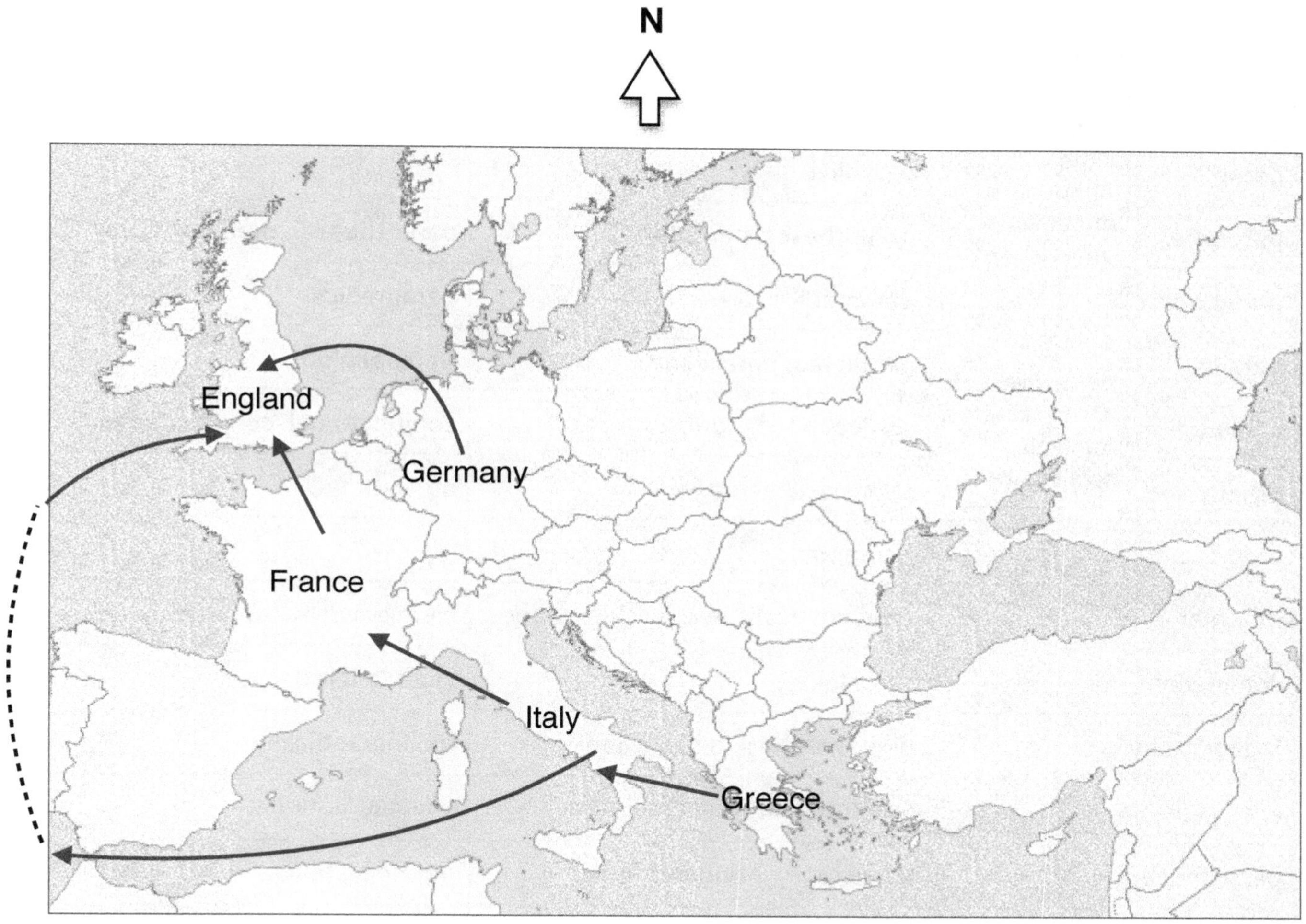

England
Germany
France
Italy
Greece

map courtesy of *Wikipedia*

Teacher Notes:
1. If you have not studied the history of the English language with your student yet, this lesson provides a great opportunity to explore that.
2. A one-page overview can be found on WG p. 174, courtesy of Mary Tanksley, our Southern CA Endorsed Trainer. The following web site also gives a concise overview of this topic. https://www.englishclub.com/english-language-history.htm
3. After studying this topic, even briefly, work through this worksheet together.

1. Take a quiz on some of your spelling words. Correct your work.
2. Add ***prefixes*** and/or ***suffixes*** to your spelling words to make ***derivatives***. All but three of them can have at least two ***derivatives***.

Prefixes	
im-	*over-*
non-	*un-*

Suffixes					
-al	*-ee*	*-(e)s*	*-ing*	*-ly*	*-ous*
-ed	*-er*	*-ic*	*-ity*	*-ness*	*-y*

Teacher Note: Although multiple options are listed for some words, only two *derivatives* are necessary for each spelling word.

Spelling Words	Derivatives	Derivatives
exquisite	exquisitely	exquisiteness
parable	parables	
parenthesis	parentheses, parenthetic	parenthetical, parenthetically
paramedic	paramedics	paramedical
parallel	paralleled, paralleling,	unparalleled
conjunction	conjunctions, nonconjunction,	conjunctional, conjunctionally
atheist	atheists	atheistic
heirloom	heirlooms	
mischief	mischievously, nonmischievously,	mischievousness, nonmischievousness
chandelier	chandeliers	chandeliered
bibliography	bibliographies, bibliographic,	bibliographically
enthusiasm	overenthusiastic, unenthusiastic,	unenthusiastically
persistence	persistency, nonpersistency,	nonpersistence
kilometer	kilometers	kilometric, kilometrical
geography	geographies, geographic,	geographically
mortal	mortally, immortal, mortality,	immortality
mortician	morticians	
mortgage	mortgages, overmortgaged,	mortgaged, mortgaging, mortgagee
kindergarten	kindergartens	kindergartener

1. Read the words in the first column. Do you know which of your spelling words are the ***antonyms*** or ***opposites***? Fill those in on your own. If you don't know them all, continue to the next step.
2. Listen as your teacher reads the List Y-2 spelling words to you slowly. Match the ***antonyms*** to your spelling words and write them on the correct line.

Antonyms	Spelling Words
add	eliminate
insult	apology
success	failure
ordinary	extraordinary
unacceptable	appropriate
murderer	martyr
stranger	acquaintance

Teacher Note:
Read all the words from List Y-2, ***in the order they occur in the WG***, having your student match the words with their appropriate *antonyms* or *synonyms.* **See note below.**

3. Read the words in the first column. Do you know which of your spelling words are the ***synonyms*** or another word that has a ***similar meaning***? Fill those in on your own. If you don't know them all, continue to the next step.
4. Listen as your teacher reads the List Y-2 spelling words to you slowly. Match the ***synonyms*** to your spelling words and write them on the correct line.

Synonyms	Spelling Words
graveyard	cemetery
doctor	physician
perseverance	endurance
adequate	sufficient
exhaustion	fatigue
calm	tranquil
try	endeavor
glass	porcelain

Teacher Note:
Having the student listen for both *opposites* **and** *similar meanings* at the same time can be challenging. You might instead read the words two times so he can focus on one language task at a time.

1. Take a quiz on some of your spelling words. Correct your work.
2. Add ***prefixes***, ***suffixes***, or both at the same time to your spelling words to make ***derivatives***. Some words can even have more than one ***suffix***.
3. If you are not sure whether a combination you want to make is a real word, look it up in the dictionary.

Prefixes	
in-	*poly-*
mono-	*re-*

Suffixes				
-al	*-ed*	*-ing*	*-ity*	*-izer*
-dom	*-es*	*-ion*	*-ize*	*-ly*

Spelling Words	Derivatives	Derivatives
martyr	martyrdom	martyred
cemetery	cemeteries	cemeterial
acquaintance	acquaintances	reacquaintance
tranquil	*tranquilize, *tranquilizer,	tranquillity, tranquilly
apology	apologies	apologize
syllable	monosyllable	polysyllable
appropriate	appropriately, inappropriate	appropriation
eliminate	elimination, eliminating,	eliminated
singe	** singeing, **singes,	singed
sufficient	sufficiently, insufficient,	insufficiently
fatigue	fatiguing	fatigued
environment	environmental	environmentally

Teacher Note: Although multiple options are listed for some words, only two *derivatives* are necessary for each spelling word.

Teacher Notes:
*The accent is on the first syllable, so these are *not* 2-1-1 words.

** Keep the E in the derivative to keep the meaning and to differentiate it from *sings* or *singing*. See SWR p. 146 #2.

4. Write a sentence using one of your new ***derivatives***.

Answers will vary.

Examples: Please accept my apologies for not having dinner ready in time.

We have many environmental issues to settle.

List Z-1 Derivatives **ANSWER KEY**

1. Take a quiz on some of your spelling words. Correct your work.
2. Add ***prefixes***, ***suffixes,*** or both at the same time to your spelling words to make ***derivatives***. Some words can even have more than one ***suffix***.
3. If you are not sure whether a combination you want to make is a real word, look it up in the dictionary.

Prefixes		
-in	*pre-*	*un-*
non-	*re-*	*under-*

Suffixes					
-able	*-ary*	*-cy*	*-ible*	*-ly*	*-ness*
-al	*-ation*	*-ed*	*-ing*	*-ment*	*-s*

Spelling Words	Derivatives	Derivatives
discern	discernible, undiscernible,	undiscernibly, discerns
	discerned, undiscerned, discernment	discerningly, undiscerningly
humorous	nonhumorous, humorousness	humorously
guarantee	guaranteed, guaranteeing,	guaranteeable, guarantees
privilege	privileged, privileging, privileges,	unprivileged, underpriviliged
recommend	recommended, recommending,	recommendation, recommends
dispense	dispensary, dispensed, dispenses,	dispensable, dispensation
combust	combustible, noncombustible,	incombustible, combusts
incessant	incessantly, incessancy,	incessantness
occurrence	reoccurrence, occurrences,	preoccurrence

Teacher Note: Although multiple options are listed for some words, only two *derivatives* are necessary for each spelling word.

4. Write a sentence using one of your new ***derivatives***.

Answers will vary.

Examples: There was no discernible difference between the two contestants.

His recommendation led to the businessman receiving the award.

1. Take a quiz on some of your spelling words in the first column. Correct your work.
2. In the second column write the ***part of speech*** each of these words can be used for, using the following codes.

   Noun **ADJ**ective **V**erb

3. A ***derivative*** is a word that is made from a ***base*** word. Write the ***base word*** for each of your spelling words in the third column. If you're not sure what it is, look it up in the dictionary.
4. Did the ***part of speech*** change? Write the new ***part of speech*** in the last column.
5. Sometimes a word can fill the role of more than one ***part of speech***. Be sure to include each case.

Spelling Words (Derivatives)	Parts of Speech	Root Words	Parts of Speech
occurrence	N	occur	V
discipline	V, N	disciple	V, N
embarrassment	N	embarrass	V
procrastination	N	procrastinate	V
recommend	V	commend	V
humorous	ADJ	humor	V, N
penitentiary	N	penitent	ADJ
incessant	ADJ	cease	V

1. A ***synonym*** is a word that has a ***similar meaning*** as another word. For example, *humorous & amusing* and *villain & scoundrel* are ***synonyms***.
2. Read the words in the first column. Do you know what they mean? Can you match them with your spelling words that are the ***synonyms***? Write them in the right column. If you don't know them all, continue to #3.
3. Listen as your teacher reads your spelling words to you slowly. Write the remaining spelling words next to their ***synonyms***.

Synonyms	Spelling Words
fish bowl	aquarium
orchestra	symphony
kingship	sovereignty
strife	dissension
writing paper	stationery
praise the Lord	hallelujah
loyalty	allegiance
assistant	lieutenant
watch	surveillance
excellence	proficiency
keepsake	souvenir
disinfectant	antiseptic

4. Write a sentence using one of the ***synonyms*** listed above and then rewrite the sentence using the spelling word that has the ***same meaning***. You'll have two sentences with ***similar*** meanings when you're done. Underline the ***synonyms*** in each sentence.

Answers will vary.

Examples: I need to buy some more writing paper so I can write some notes to my family.

I need to buy some more stationery so I can write some notes to my family.

1. Many of your spelling words from List Z-2 is derived from either ***Latin or Greek***. Read through the ***roots*** and their meanings below.
2. As you take a quiz on your spelling words, match them to their ***roots***. Write the words in the appropriate column and on the correct line. Three of the words are listed twice. Correct your work.

Latin Roots	Meanings	English
facere	to make	proficiency
manu	hand	maneuver
sensio	think, feel	dissension
tenere	hold	lieutenant
veiller	watch	surveillance
venire	come to mind	souvenir

Greek Roots	Meanings	English
anti-	against	antiseptic
aqua	water	aquarium
chronos	time	synchronize
hippos	horse	hippopotamus
phon	sound	symphony
pneuma	breathe	pneumonia
potamos	river	hippopotamus
rhino	nose	rhinoceros
syn	together, like	symphony
		synonym
		synchronize

1. Long English words are nothing but short syllables made of ***phonograms*** and which use our ***spelling rules***. Once you start recognizing the ***roots*** in words, the meanings also becomes clear.

2. As your teacher dictates it, write one of the longest words in the English language here. Add the markings.

pneu mo no ul tra mi cro scop ic sil i co vol ca no co ni o sis

> **Teacher Note:** Use full spelling dictation for this word. Because of its length, you'll want to break it down into segments such as ***pneu mo no*** + ***ul tra*** + ... Have the student dictate it back to you and then add markings before completing the rest.

3. Wow! What a long word!
   a. How many syllables does this word have? 19 How many letters? 45

4. When we take a closer look, we see some facts that make this word much more manageable.
   a. How many multi-letter phonograms does it have? 2
   b. How many rules is it using? 3 (#2, 4, and 5)
   c. How many letters are saying their first sound? 31
   d. That means that for every 3 letters, 2 of them are saying their first sound, and the rest are following predictable and reliable rules that help us know what they say.

5. Use the ***roots*** and their meanings listed below to figure out what this medical word means.

a lung disease caused by very small silica dust particles

> **Teacher Note:** Accept any reasonable attempt at a definition for this word.

Greek Roots	Meanings
pneumono	lung
micro	very small
skopós	to look at
konis	dust
-osis	abnormal condition or state; a disorder

Latin Roots	Meanings
ultra	beyond
-ic	having the characteristics of, like
silica	silicon dioxide; powder used to make glass
volcanus	an opening that erupts

CPSIA information can be obtained
at www.ICGtesting.com
Printed in the USA
FSHW02n1548051018
52674FS

9 780974 492032